Henry Lawson

TREASURY

ILLUSTRATED BY

Oslo Davis

RANDOM HOUSE AUSTRALIA

A Random House book
Published by Random House Australia Pty Ltd
Level 3, 100 Pacific Highway, North Sydney NSW 2060
www.randomhouse.com.au

First published by Random House Australia in 2014

Illustration copyright © Oslo Davis 2014

The moral right of the author and illustrator has been asserted.

Addresses for companies within the Random House Group can be found at
www.randomhouse.com.au/offices

National Library of Australia
Cataloguing-in-Publication Entry
Author: Lawson, Henry, 1867-1922, author.
Title: Henry Lawson treasury / Henry Lawson; Oslo Davis, illustrator.
ISBN: 9780857985132 (paperback)
Subjects: Australian poetry. Ballads – Australia.Short stories, Australian.
Other Authors/Contributors: Davis, Oslo, illustrator.

Cover and internal illustrations by Oslo Davis
Cover and internal design by Christa Moffitt, Christbella Designs
Typeset in Bembo 12/22
Printed in China by 1010 Printing International Co.

Random House Australia uses papers that are natural, renewable and recyclable products and made
from wood grown in sustainable forests. The logging and manufacturing processes are expected to
conform to the environmental regulations of the country of origin

CONTENTS

About

HENRY LAWSON (1867-1922)

Henry Lawson is one of Australia's most celebrated literary icons. He is best known for his poems, ballads and short stories such as 'The Drover's Wife' and 'The Loaded Dog'. Lawson was known throughout his career as 'The Poet of the People' and he is still considered one of our greatest ever short story writers.

Lawson was born on the Grenfell goldfields in New South Wales on 17 June 1867. His family later moved to a small farm in Gulgong, in the Mudgee district. Lawson didn't attend school until he was nine years old because there was no local schoolhouse before that time. Not long after he started school, Henry developed an ear infection and began to lose his hearing. By the time he was 14, Lawson was almost completely deaf and was forced to leave school.

In 1883 Lawson's parents separated and his mother, Louisa, moved to Sydney. Henry joined her in the city later that year and got an apprenticeship with a coach painter. He also started taking night classes to finish his schooling. It was around this time that Lawson began writing fiction and poetry.

Lawson's first poem, 'A Song of the Republic', was published in *The Bulletin* magazine in October 1887 and reflected his strong political views. He also began his journalism career at this time, writing pieces for *The Republican*, which was co-founded by his mother. Within a few years, Lawson had developed a reputation as a popular writer of both poetry and prose.

Throughout the next few years Lawson was a regular contributor to popular publications of the time such as *Boomerang, Worker* and *The Bulletin*. He also began writing short stories, including 'The Drover's Wife', which remains one of Australia's most iconic pieces of writing and documents the hardships faced by many Australians trying to make a living in the outback.

In 1892, *The Bulletin* offered Lawson an assignment to Bourke in the north-west of New South Wales to report on the drought that was affecting much of New South Wales. This trip had a big impact on Lawson's life and writing. The hardships and poverty Lawson witnessed in the outback were the basis for many of his future stories.

Lawson's book *Short Stories in Poems and Verse* was published in 1894. Many of the stories, such as 'The Bush Undertaker' and 'The Union Buries its Dead', were inspired by his trip Bourke and its surrounding regions. Unlike other writers of the time, such as Banjo

Paterson, Lawson did not have a romantic idea of the Australian bush. Instead, he wrote about the harsh realities of bush life.

Lawson's first major, and most popular, short story collection was published two years later. It was titled *When the Billy Boils* and contained stories such as 'The Drover's Wife,' which remain iconic today. Despite his success, Lawson struggled with personal issues, such as alcoholism.

In the same year *When the Billy Boils* was published, Lawson married Bertha Bredt. The couple had two children, Joseph and Bertha. The family moved to London in 1900, where Lawson continued to write. He had two books published, *Joe Wilson and his Mates* and *Children of the Bus*. Despite this, neither Henry nor Bertha was happy. Bertha was hospitalised for depression in 1901 and the family returned to Australia in 1902. The following year the couple separated.

Lawson continued to write and had three books published between 1910 and 1915, including *The Skyline Riders and other Verses My Army, o my Army! and other Songs* and *Triangles of Life and other stories*. Despite this, he continued to struggle. He often had trouble paying his bills and was admitted to mental institutions on several occasions.

Henry Lawson died in Sydney in 1922.

A Song
OF THE REPUBLIC

Sons of the South, awake! arise!

    Sons of the South, and do.

Banish from under your bonny skies

Those old-world errors and wrongs and lies.

Making a hell in a Paradise

    That belongs to your sons and you.

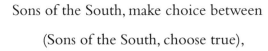

Sons of the South, make choice between

    (Sons of the South, choose true),

The Land of Morn and the Land of E'en,

The Old Dead Tree and the Young Tree Green,

The Land that belongs to the lord and the Queen,

    And the Land that belongs to you.

Sons of the South, *your* time will come –

    Sons of the South, 'tis near –

The 'Signs of the Times', in their language dumb,

Fortell it, and ominous whispers hum

Like sullen sounds of a distant drum,

    In the ominous atmosphere.

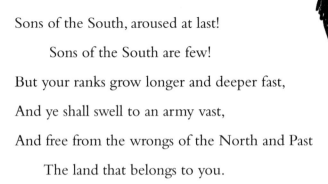

Sons of the South, aroused at last!

    Sons of the South are few!

But your ranks grow longer and deeper fast,

And ye shall swell to an army vast,

And free from the wrongs of the North and Past

    The land that belongs to you.

First published in *The Bulletin*, 1 October 1887

Andy's GONE WITH CATTLE

Our Andy's gone to battle now
   'Gainst Drought, the red marauder;
Our Andy's gone with cattle now
   Across the Queensland border.

He's left us in dejection now;
   Our hearts with him are roving.
It's dull on this selection now,
   Since Andy went a-droving.

Who now shall wear the cheerful face
   In times when things are slackest?
And who shall whistle round the place
   When Fortune frowns her blackest?

Oh, who shall cheek the squatter now
 When he comes round us snarling?
His tongue is growing hotter now
 Since Andy cross'd the Darling.

The gates are out of order now,
 Each wind the riders rattle;
For far far across the border now
 Our Andy's gone with cattle.

Poor Aunty's looking thin and white;
 And Uncle's cross with worry;
And poor old Blucher howls all night
 Since Andy left Macquarie.

Oh, may the showers in torrents fall,
  And all the tanks run over;
And may the grass grow green and tall
  In pathways of the drover;

And may good angels send the rain
  On desert stretches sandy;
And when the summer comes again
  God grant 'twill bring us Andy.

First published in *Australian Town and Country Journal*,
13 October 1888

Faces
IN THE STREET

They lie, the men who tell us in a loud decisive tone

That want is here a stranger, and that misery's unknown;

For where the nearest suburb and the city proper meet

My window-sill is level with the faces in the street —

    Drifting past, drifting past,

    To the beat of weary feet —

While I sorrow for the owners of those faces in the street.

And cause I have to sorrow, in a land so young and fair,

To see upon those faces stamped the marks of Want and Care;

I look in vain for traces of the fresh and fair and sweet

In sallow, sunken faces that are drifting through the street —

    Drifting on, drifting on,

    To the scrape of restless feet;

I can sorrow for the owners of the faces in the street.

In hours before the dawning dims the starlight in the sky

The wan and weary faces first begin to trickle by,

Increasing as the moments hurry on with morning feet,

Till like a pallid river flow the faces in the street —

  Flowing in, flowing in,

  To the beat of hurried feet —

Ah! I sorrow for the owners of those faces in the street.

The human river dwindles when 'tis past the hour of eight,

Its waves go flowing faster in the fear of being late;

But slowly drag the moments, whilst beneath the dust and heat

The city grinds the owners of the faces in the street —

  Grinding body, grinding soul,

  Yielding scarce enough to eat —

Oh! I sorrow for the owners of the faces in the street.

And then the only faces till the sun is sinking down

Are those of outside toilers and the idlers of the town,

Save here and there a face that seems a stranger in the street,

Tells of the city's unemployed upon his weary beat —

  Drifting round, drifting round,

  To the tread of listless feet —

Ah! My heart aches for the owner of that sad face in the street.

And when the hours on lagging feet have slowly dragged away,

And sickly yellow gaslights rise to mock the going day,

Then flowing past my window like a tide in its retreat,

Again I see the pallid stream of faces in the street —

   Ebbing out, ebbing out,

   To the drag of tired feet,

While my heart is aching dumbly for the faces in the street.

And now all blurred and smirched with vice the day's sad pages end,

For while the short 'large hours' toward the longer 'small hours' trend,

With smiles that mock the wearer, and with words that half entreat,

Delilah pleads for custom at the corner of the street —

   Sinking down, sinking down,

   Battered wreck by tempests beat —

A dreadful, thankless trade is hers, that Woman of the Street.

But, ah! to dreader things than these our fair young city comes,

For in its heart are growing thick the filthy dens and slums,

Where human forms shall rot away in sties for swine unmeet,

And ghostly faces shall be seen unfit for any street —

   Rotting out, rotting out,

   For the lack of air and meat —

In dens of vice and horror that are hidden from the street.

I wonder would the apathy of wealthy men endure

Were all their windows level with the faces of the Poor?

Ah! Mammon's slaves, your knees shall knock, your hearts in terror beat,

When God demands a reason for the sorrows of the street,

  The wrong things and the bad things

  And the sad things that we meet

In the filthy lane and alley, and the cruel, heartless street.

I left the dreadful corner where the steps are never still,

And sought another window overlooking gorge and hill;

But when the night came dreary with the driving rain and sleet,

They haunted me – the shadows of those faces in the street,

  Flitting by, flitting by,

  Flitting by with noiseless feet,

And with cheeks but little paler than the real ones in the street.

Once I cried: 'Oh, God Almighty! if Thy might doth still endure,

Now show me in a vision for the wrongs of Earth a cure.'

And, lo! with shops all shuttered I beheld a city's street,

And in the warning distance heard the tramp of many feet,

   Coming near, coming near,

   To a drum's dull distant beat,

And soon I saw the army that was marching down the street.

Then, like a swollen river that has broken bank and wall,

The human flood came pouring with the red flags over all,

And kindled eyes all blazing bright with revolution's heat,

And flashing swords reflecting rigid faces in the street.

   Pouring on, pouring on,

   To a drum's loud threatening beat,

And the war-hymns and the cheering of the people in the street.

And so it must be while the world goes rolling round its course,

The warning pen shall write in vain, the warning voice grow hoarse,

But not until a city feels Red Revolution's feet

Shall its sad people miss awhile the terrors of the street –

  The dreadful everlasting strife

  For scarcely clothes and meat

In that pent track of living death – the city's cruel street.

First published in *The Bulletin*, 28 July 1888

The
BLUE MOUNTAINS

Above the ashes straight and tall,
 Through ferns with moisture dripping,
I climb beneath the sandstone wall,
 My feet on mosses slipping.

Like ramparts round the valley's edge
 The tinted cliffs are standing,
With many a broken wall and ledge,
 And many a rock landing.

And round about their rugged feet
 Deep ferny dells are hidden
In shadowed depths, whence dust and heat
 Are banished and forbidden.

The stream that, crooning to itself,
 Comes down a tireless rover,
Flows calmly to the rocky shelf,
 And there leaps bravely over.

Now pouring down, now lost in spray
 When mountain breezes sally
The water strikes the rock midway,
 And leaps into the valley.

Now in the west the colours change,

The blue with crimson blending;

Behind the far Dividing Range,

The sun is fast descending.

And mellowed day comes o'er the place,

And softens ragged edges;

The rising moon's great placid face

Looks gravely o'er the ledges.

First published in 1888

A
NEGLECTED HISTORY

We must admit that the Centennial celebrations in Sydney were not wholly useless. The glorious occasion called forth from every daily, weekly and monthly periodical, every advertising medium, twopenny calendar, and centennial keepsake, a more or less complete history of Australian progress during the past 100 years. The youngsters in our schools, and Australians generally, had thus for the first time the salient facts regarding the history of Australia thrust before them.

If this is Australia, and not a mere outlying suburb of England: if we really are the nucleus of a nation and not a mere handful of expatriated people dependent on an English Colonial Secretary for guidance and tuition, it behoves us to educate our children to a knowledge of the country they call their own.

It is a matter of public shame that while we have now commemorated our hundredth anniversary, not one in every ten children attending Public schools throughout the colonies is acquainted with a single historical fact about Australia.

The children are taught more of the meanest state in Europe than of the country they are born and bred in, despite the singularity of its characteristics, the interest of its history, the rapidity of its advance, and the stupendous promise of its future.

They can conjure with the name of Captain Cook; they are aware that he sailed into Botany Bay, and they have some indistinct theories regarding him, but of the men who in the past fought for the freedom of our constitution as it is, they scarcely know the names.

It is of course desirable that they should be familiar with the features of European history, but that they should at the same time be so grossly unacquainted with their native land is an obvious anomaly.

Select almost any Australian schoolboy from one of the higher classes and you will find that he can glibly recite the names of the English sovereigns from the Conqueror to Victoria, with the dates of their ascension. He can then give you their relationship to each other, and the principal events and noteworthy persons of each reign, with a rapidity that runs clear away from elocution and transmutes the English language into a kind of lightning gibberish. If you ask for geographical information he can quote, without drawing breath, the rivers, mountains and towns in Europe, and can then run through the counties and towns of England, repeating such names as Kent, Surrey, Sussex, Berkshire, Hampshire, Wiltshire, etc., with a great relish. But if you ask him what town in Australia was formerly called Bendigo, or where Port Phillip settlement was, he becomes bashfully silent, and if you follow this by inquiries as to the Black War in Tasmania, or ask him the causes which led to the Fight of Vinegar Hill, he will come to the conclusion that you are 'greening' him, and will leave with an injured air.

Of the gradual separation of one colony from another, of
the differences still existing in their constitutions, and of the men
and influences which have made them what they are he knows
nothing. His knowledge of the natural history and geographical
features of Australasia he picks up chiefly from the talk of his
associates, and the information he casually encounters in the
newspapers.

It is quite time that our children were taught a little more
about their country, for shame's sake. Are they always to be
'Colonials' and not 'Australians'?

It may be urged that the early history of Australia is for
the most part better left unknown; but for that reason are all
the bright spots, the clean pages, the good deeds, and the noble
names, to be left unremembered too?

There is apparently quite another reason why Australian history may not claim a place in the school's curriculum. It is considered necessary that a loyal spirit should be instilled into the minds of the rising generation: an attachment to a mother land which they have never seen: a 'home' which should remain always dearer to them than the place of their birth and childhood. This object might be considerably retarded if the children learned how the mother land cradled and nursed the nation they belonged to, and the measure of gratitude and respect they owe her for her tender guardianship: if they knew how the present Australian aristocracy (so loyal and sceptre loving) arose, and whence they came; how the Old New South Wales convict slaveholders and tyrants tried to drag Victoria into the sewer while she made efforts for liberty; how the same worthies tried to divert a convict stream into the northern settlement (now Queensland) that they might reap the benefit of convict labour; if the noble efforts of Lang resulted in the freedom of the mother colony, and lastly how Australian honour and interests were sold right and left for mammon.

If all these things, and much more that might and would become apparent, were taught, Australian school children might develop a spirit totally at variance with the wishes of Australian Groveldom.

They might form a low admiration for the thirty digger patriots, who on that eventful December morning in 1854 died in the Eureka Stockade to gain a juster government for their country and to baulk the first 'try on' of what was no less than convict government in a free colony. They might also learn to love the blue flag with the white cross, that bonny 'Flag of the Southern Cross', which only rose once, but rose to mark the brightest spot in Australian history, and to give a severe check to that high-handed government which is only now gaining ground again.

They might acquire a preference for some national and patriotic song of their own homes and their own appointed rulers, rather than to stand in a row and squeal, in obedience to custom and command, 'God Save our Gracious Queen'.

In their present state of blissful compulsory ignorance they cannot perceive the foolishness of singing praises of the graciousness of their condescending magnate, a ruler at the further end of the world who, knowing as little of them and their lives and aspirations as they know of her, is nevertheless their sovereign and potentate, and who is sometimes benevolent enough to send them a brief cable message judiciously filtered through her own appointed underling and deputy.

When the school children of Australia are told more truths about their own country, and fewer lies about the virtues of Royalty, the day will be near when we can place our own national flag in one of the proudest places among the ensigns of the world.

First published in *The Republican*, 4 April 1888

The TEAMS

A cloud of dust on the long white road,
  And the teams go creeping on
Inch by inch with the weary load;
And by the power of the greenhide goad
  The distant goal is won.

With eyes half-shut from the blinding dust,
  And necks to the yokes bent low,
The beasts are pulling as bullocks must;
And the shining tires might also rust
  While the spokes are turning slow.

With face half hid 'neath a wide brimmed hat

   That shades from the heat's white waves,

And shouldered whip with its green-hide plait,

The driver plods with a gait like that

   Of his weary, patient slaves.

He wipes his brow, for the day is hot,

   And spits to the left with spite;

He shouts at 'Bally,' and flicks at 'Scot',

And raises dust from the back of 'Spot',

   And spits to the dusty right.

He'll sometimes pause as a thing of form
    In front of a settler's door,
And ask for a drink, and remark "It's warm,'
Or say 'There's signs of a thunderstorm;'
    But he seldom utters more.

But, ah! there are other scenes than these;
   And, passing his lonely home,
For weeks together the bushman sees
The teams bogg'd down o'er the axletrees,
   Or ploughing the sodden loam.

And then when the roads are at their worst,
   The bushman's children hear
The cruel blows of the whips revers'd
While bullocks pull as their hearts would burst,
   And bellow with pain and fear.

And thus with little of joy or rest
   Are the long, long journeys done;
And thus – 'tis a cruel war at the best
Is distance fought in the lonely west,
   And the lonely battles won.

First published in *The Australian Town and Country Journal*,
21 December 1889

The DROVER'S SWEETHEART

An hour before the sun goes down

  Behind the ragged boughs,

I go across the little run

  And bring the dusty cows;

And once I used to sit and rest

  Beneath the fading dome,

For there was one that I loved best

  Who'd bring the cattle home.

Our yard is fixed with double bails,
  Round one the grass is green,
The bush is growing through the rails,
  The spike is rusted in;
And 'twas from there his freckled face
  Would turn and smile at me –
He'd milk a dozen in the race
  While I was milking three.

I milk eleven cows myself
  Where once I milked but four;
I set the dishes on the shelf
  And close the dairy door;
And when the glaring sunlight fails
  And the fire shines through the cracks,
I climb the broken stockyard rails
  And watch the bridle-tracks.

He kissed me twice and once again

 And rode across the hill,

The pint-pots and the hobble-chain

 I hear them jingling still;

He'll come at night or not at all –

 He left in dust and heat,

And when the soft, cool shadows fall

 Is the best time to meet.

And he is coming back again,

    He wrote to let me know,

The floods were in the Darling then –

    It seems so long ago;

He'd come through miles of slush and mud,

    And it was weary work,

The creeks were bankers, and the flood

    Was forty miles round Bourke.

He said the floods had formed a block,

    The plains could not be crossed,

And there was foot-rot in the flock

    And hundreds had been lost;

The sheep were falling thick and fast

    A hundred miles from town,

And when he reached the line at last

    He trucked the remnant down.

And so he'll have to stand the cost;
     His luck was always bad,
Instead of making more, he lost
     The money that he had;
And how he'll manage, heaven knows
     (My eyes are getting dim),
He says – he says – he don't – suppose
     I'll want – to – marry – him.

As if I wouldn't take his hand
     Without a golden glove –
Oh! Jack, you men won't understand
     How much a girl can love.
I long to see his face once more –
     Jack's dog! thank God, it's Jack! –
(I never thought I'd faint before)
     He's coming – up – the track.

First published in *The Boomerang*, 20 June 1891

Freedom
ON THE WALLABY

Australia's a big country
   An' Freedom's humping bluey,
An' Freedom's on the wallaby
   Oh! don't you hear 'er cooey?
She's just begun to boomerang,
   She'll knock the tyrants silly,
She's goin' to light another fire
   And boil another billy.

Our fathers toiled for bitter bread
　　While loafers thrived beside 'em,
But food to eat and clothes to wear,
　　Their native land denied 'em.
An' so they left their native land
　　In spite of their devotion,
An' so they came, or if they stole,
　　Were sent across the ocean.

Then Freedom couldn't stand the glare
　　O' Royalty's regalia,
She left the loafers where they were,
　　An' came out to Australia.
But now across the mighty main
　　The chains have come ter bind her –
She little thought to see again
　　The wrongs she left behind her.

Our parents toil'd to make a home -
   Hard grubbin 'twas an' clearin' -
They wasn't crowded much with lords
   When they was pioneering.
But now that we have made the land
   A garden full of promise,
Old Greed must crook 'is dirty hand
   And come ter take it from us.

So we must fly a rebel flag,
   As others did before us,
And we must sing a rebel song
   And join in rebel chorus.
We'll make the tyrants feel the sting
   O' those that they would throttle;
They needn't say the fault is ours
   If blood should stain the wattle!

First published in *The Worker*, 16 May 1891

The
DROVER'S WIFE

The two-roomed house is built of round timber, slabs, and stringy-bark, and floored with split slabs. A big bark kitchen standing at one end is larger than the house itself, veranda included.

Bush all round – bush with no horizon, for the country is flat. No ranges in the distance. The bush consists of stunted, rotten native apple trees. No undergrowth. Nothing to relieve the eye save the darker green of a few she-oaks which are sighing above the narrow, almost waterless creek. Nineteen miles to the nearest sign of civilisation – a shanty on the main road.

The drover, an ex-squatter, is away with sheep. His wife and children are left here alone.

Four ragged, dried-up-looking children are playing about the house. Suddenly one of them yells: 'Snake! Mother, here's a snake!'

The gaunt, sun-browned bushwoman dashes from the kitchen, snatches her baby from the ground, holds it on her left hip, and reaches for a stick.

'Where is it?'

'Here! Gone in the wood-heap!;' yells the eldest boy – a sharp-faced urchin of eleven. 'Stop there, mother! I'll have him. Stand back! I'll have the beggar!'

'Tommy, come here, or you'll be bit. Come here at once when I tell you, you little wretch!'

The youngster comes reluctantly, carrying a stick bigger than himself. Then he yells, triumphantly:

'There it goes – under the house!' and darts away with club uplifted. At the same time the big, black, yellow-eyed dog-of-all-breeds, who has shown the wildest interest in the proceedings, breaks his chain and rushes after that snake. He is a moment late, however, and his nose reaches the crack in the slabs just as the end of its tail disappears. Almost at the same moment the boy's club comes down and skins the aforesaid nose. Alligator takes small notice of this, and proceeds to undermine the building; but he is subdued after a struggle and chained up. They cannot afford to lose him.

The drover's wife makes the children stand together near the dog-house while she watches for the snake. She gets two small dishes of milk and sets them down near the wall to tempt it to come out; but an hour goes by and it does not show itself.

It is near sunset, and a thunderstorm is coming. The children must be brought inside. She will not take them into the house, for she knows the snake is there, and may at any moment come up through a crack in the rough slab floor; so she carries several armfuls of firewood into the kitchen, and then takes the children there. The kitchen has no floor – or, rather, an earthen one – called a 'ground floor' in this part of the bush. There is a large, roughly-made table in the centre of the place. She brings the children in, and makes them get on this table. They are two boys and two girls – mere babies. She gives them some supper, and then, before it gets dark, she goes into house, and snatches up some pillows and bedclothes – expecting to see or lay or hand on the snake any minute. She makes a bed on the kitchen table for the children, and sits down beside it to watch all night.

She has an eye on the corner, and a green sapling club laid in readiness on the dresser by her side; also her sewing basket and a copy of the *Young Ladies' Journal*. She has brought the dog into the room.

Tommy turns in, under protest, but says he'll lie awake all night and smash that blinded snake.

His mother asks him how many times she has told not to swear.

He has his club with him under the bedclothes, and Jacky protests:

'Mummy! Tommy's skinnin' me alive wif his club. Make him take it out.'

Tommy: 'Shet up you little – ! D'yer want to be bit with the snake?'

Jacky shuts up.

'If yer bit,' says Tommy, after a pause, 'you'll swell up, an smell, an' turn red an' green an' blue all over till yer bust. Won't he mother?'

'Now then, don't frighten the child. Go to sleep,' she says.

The two younger children go to sleep, and now and then Jacky complains of being 'skeezed.' More room is made for him. Presently Tommy says: 'Mother! Listen to them (adjective) little possums. I'd like to screw their blanky necks.'

And Jacky protests drowsily.

'But they don't hurt us, the little blanks!'

Mother: 'There, I told you you'd teach Jacky to swear.' But the remark makes her smile. Jacky goes to sleep.

Presently Tommy asks:

'Mother! Do you think they'll ever extricate the (adjective) kangaroo?'

'Lord! How am I to know, child? Go to sleep.'

'Will you wake me if the snake comes out?'

'Yes. Go to sleep.'

Near midnight. The children are all asleep and she sits there still, sewing and reading by turns. From time to time she glances round the floor and wall-plate, and, whenever she hears a noise, she reaches for the stick. The thunderstorm comes on, and the wind, rushing through the cracks in the slab wall, threatens to blow out her candle. She places it on a sheltered part of the dresser and fixes

up a newspaper to protect it. At every flash of lightning, the cracks between the slabs gleam like polished silver. The thunder rolls, and the rain comes down in torrents.

Alligator lies at full length on the floor, with his eyes turned towards the partition. She knows by this that the snake is there. There are large cracks in that wall opening under the floor of the dwelling-house.

She is not a coward, but recent events have shaken her nerves. A little son of her brother-in-law was lately bitten by a snake, and died. Besides, she has not heard from her husband for six months, and is anxious about him.

He was a drover, and started squatting here when they were married. The drought of 18 – ruined him. He had to sacrifice the remnant of his flock and go droving again. He intends to move his family into the nearest town when he comes back, and, in the meantime, his brother, who keeps a shanty on the main road, comes over about once a month with provisions. The wife has still a couple of cows, one horse, and a few sheep. The brother-in-law kills one of the latter occasionally, gives her what she needs of it, and takes the rest in return for other provisions.

She is used to being left alone. She once lived like this for eighteen months. As a girl she built the usual castles in the air; but all her girlish hopes and aspirations have long been dead. She finds all the excitement and recreation she needs in the *Young Ladies' Journal*, and Heaven help her! Takes a pleasure in the fashion plates.

Her husband is an Australian, and so is she. He is careless, but a good enough husband. If he had the means he would take her to the city and keep her there like a princess. They are used to being apart, or at least she is. 'No use fretting,' she says. He may forget sometimes that he is married; but if he has a good cheque when he comes back he will give most of it to her. When he had money he took her to the city several times – hired a railway sleeping compartment, and put up at the best hotels. He also bought her a buggy, but they had to sacrifice that along with the rest.

The last two children were born in the bush – one while her husband was bringing a drunken doctor, by force, to attend to her. She was alone on this occasion, and very weak. She had been ill with fever. She prayed to God to send her assistance. God sent Black Mary – the 'whitest' gin in all the land. Or, at least, God sent King Jimmy first, and he sent Black Mary. He put his black face round the door post, took in the situation at a glance, and said cheerfully: 'All right, missus – I bring my old woman, she down alonga creek.'

One of the children died while she was here alone. She rode nineteen miles for assistance, carrying the dead child.

It must be near one or two o'clock. The fire is burning low. Alligator lies with his head resting on his paws, and watches the wall. He is not a very beautiful dog, and the light shows numerous old wounds where the hair will not grow. He is afraid of nothing on the face of the earth or under it. He will tackle a bullock as readily as he will tackle a flea. He hates all other dogs – except kangaroo-dogs – and has a marked dislike to friends or relations of the family. They seldom call, however. He sometimes makes friends with strangers. He hates snakes and has killed many, but he will be bitten some day and die; most snake-dogs end that way.

Now and then the bushwoman lays down her work and watches, and listens, and thinks. She thinks of things in her own life, for there is little else to think about.

The rain will make the grass grow, and this reminds her how she fought a bush-fire once while her husband was away. The grass was long, and very dry, and the fire threatened to burn her out. She put on an old pair of her husband's trousers and beat out the flames with a green bough, till great drops of sooty perspiration stood out on her forehead and ran in streaks down her blackened arms. The sight of his mother in trousers greatly amused Tommy, who worked like a little hero by her side, but the terrified baby howled lustily for his 'mummy.' The fire would have mastered her but for four excited bushmen who arrived in the nick of time. It was a mixed-up affair all round; when she went to take up the baby he screamed and struggled convulsively, thinking it was a 'blackman;' and Alligator, trusting more to the child's sense than his own instinct, charged furiously, and (being old and slightly deaf) did not in his excitement at first recognise his mistress's voice, but continued to hang on to the moleskins until choked off by Tommy with a saddle-strap. The dog's sorrow for his blunder, and his anxiety to let it be known that it was all a mistake, was as evident as his ragged tail and a twelve-inch grin could make it. It was a glorious time for the boys; a day to look back to, and talk about, and laugh over for many years.

She thinks how she fought a flood during her husband's absence. She stood for hours in the drenching downpour, and dug an overflow gutter to save the dam across the creek. But she could not save it. There are things that a bushwoman cannot do. Next morning the dam was broken, and her heart was nearly broken too, for she thought how her husband would feel when he came home and saw the result of years of labour swept away. She cried then.

She also fought the pleuro-pneumonia – dosed and bled the few remaining cattle, and wept again when her two best cows died.

Again, she fought a mad bullock that besieged the house for a day. She made bullets and fired at him through cracks in the slabs with an old shot-gun. He was dead in the morning. She skinned him and got seventeen-and-sixpence for the hide.

She also fights the crows and eagles that have designs on her chickens. Her plan of campaign is very original. The children cry 'Crows, mother!' and she rushes out and aims a broomstick at the birds as though it were a gun, and says 'Bung!' The crows leave in a hurry; they are cunning, but a woman's cunning is greater.

Occasionally a bushman in the horrors, or a villainous-looking sundowner, comes and nearly scares the life out of her. She generally tells the suspicious-looking stranger that her husband and two sons are at work below the dam, or over at the yard, for he always cunningly inquires for the boss.

Only last week a gallows-faced swagman – having satisfied himself that there were no men on the place – threw his swag down on the veranda, and demanded tucker. She gave him something to eat; then he expressed the intention of staying for the night. It was sundown then. She got a batten from the sofa, loosened the dog,

51

and confronted the stranger, holding the batten in one hand and the dog's collar with the other. 'Now you go!' she said. He looked at her and at the dog, said 'All right, mum,' in a cringing tone and left. She was a determined-looking woman, and Alligator's yellow eyes glared unpleasantly – besides, the dog's chawing-up apparatus greatly resembled that of the reptile he was named after.

She has few pleasures to think of as she sits here alone by the fire, on guard against a snake. All days are much the same for her; but on Sunday afternoon she dresses herself, tidies the children, smartens up baby, and goes for a lonely walk along the bush-track, pushing an old perambulator in front of her. She does this every Sunday. She takes as much care to make herself and the children look smart as she would if she were going to do the block in the city. There is nothing to see, however, and not a soul to meet. You might walk for twenty miles along this track without being able to fix a point in your mind, unless you are a bushman. This is because of the everlasting, maddening sameness of the stunted trees – that monotony which makes a man long to break away and travel as far as trains can go, and sail as far as ship can sail – and farther.

But this bushwoman is used to the loneliness of it. As a girl-wife she hated it, but now she would feel strange away from it.

She is glad when her husband returns, but she does not gush or make a fuss about it. She gets him something good to eat, and tidies up the children.

She seems contented with her lot. She loves her children, but has no time to show it. She seems harsh to them. Her surroundings are not favourable to the development of the 'womanly' or sentimental side of nature.

It must be nearing morning now; but the clock is in the dwelling-house. Her candle is nearly done; she forgot that she was out of candles. Some more wood must be got to keep the fire up, and so she shuts the dog inside and hurries around to the woodheap. The rain has cleared off. She seizes a stick, pulls it out, and – crash! The whole pile collapses.

Yesterday she bargained with a stray blackfellow to bring her some wood, and while he was at work she went in search of a missing cow. She was absent an hour or so, and the native black made good use of his time. On her return she was so astonished to see a good heap of wood by the chimney, and she gave him an extra fig of tobacco, and praised him for not being lazy. He thanked her, and left with head erect and chest well out. He was the last of his tribe and a King; but he had built that woodheap hollow.

She is hurt now, and tears spring to her eyes as she sits down again by the table. She takes up a handkerchief to wipe the tears away, but pokes her eyes with her bare fingers instead. The handkerchief is full of holes, and she finds that she has put her thumb through one, and her forefinger through another.

This makes her laugh, to the surprise of the dog. She has a keen, very keen, sense of the ridiculous; and some time or other she will amuse bushmen with the story.

She has been amused before like that. One day she sat down 'to have a good cry,' as she said – and the old cat rubbed against her dress and 'cried too.' Then she had to laugh.

It must be near daylight now. The room is very close and hot because of the fire. Alligator still watches the wall from time to time. Suddenly he becomes greatly interested; he draws himself a few inches nearer the partition, and a thrill runs through his body. The hair on the back of his neck begins to bristle, and the battle-light is in his yellow eyes. She knows what this means, and lays her hand on the stick. The lower end of one of the partition slabs has a large crack on both sides. An evil pair of small, bright bead-like eyes glisten at one of these holes. The snake – a black one – comes slowly out, about a foot, and moves its head up and down. The dog lies still, and the woman sits as one fascinated. The snake comes out a foot further. She lifts her stick, and the reptile, as though suddenly aware of danger, sticks his head in through the crack on the other side of the slab, and hurries to get his tail round after him. Alligator springs, and his jaws come together with a snap. He misses, for his nose is large, and the snake's body close down on the angle formed by the slabs and the floor. He snaps again as the tail comes round. He has the snake now, and tugs it out eighteen inches. Thud, thud. Alligator gives another pull and he has the snake out – a black brute, five feet long. The head rises to dart about, but the dog has the enemy close to the neck. He is a big, heavy dog, but quick as a terrier. He shakes the snake as though he felt the original curse in common with mankind. The eldest boy wakes up, seizes his stick, and tries to get out of bed, but his mother forces him back with a grip of iron. Thud, thud – the snake's back is broken in several places. Thud, thud – it's head is crushed, and Alligator's nose skinned again.

She lifts the mangled reptile on the point of her stick, carries it to the fire, and throws it in; then piles on the wood and watches the snake burn. The boy and the dog watch too. She lays her hand on the dog's head, and all the fierce, angry light dies out of his yellow eyes. The younger children are quieted, and presently go to sleep. The dirty-legged boy stands for a moment in his shirt, watching the fire. Presently he looks up at her, sees the tears in her eyes, and, throwing his arms around her neck exclaims:

'Mother, I won't never go drovin'; blarst me if I do!'

And she hugs him to her worn-out breast and kisses him; and they sit thus together while the sickly daylight breaks over bush.

First published in *The Bulletin,* 23 July 1892

The
CITY BUSHMAN
(in answer to 'Banjo' and otherwise)

It was pleasant up the country, City Bushman, where you went,

For you sought the greener patches and you travelled like a gent;

And you curse the trams and buses and the turmoil and the push,

Though you know the squalid city needn't keep you from the bush;

But we lately heard you singing of the 'plains where shade is not',

And you mentioned it was dusty – 'all was dry and all was hot'.

True, the bush 'hath moods and changes' – and the bushman hath 'em, too,

For he's not a poet's dummy – he's a man, the same as you;

But his back is growing rounder – slaving for the absentee –

And his toiling wife is thinner than a country wife should be.

For we noticed that the faces of the folks we chanced to meet

Should have made a greater contrast to the faces in the street;

And, in short, we think the bushman's being driven to the wall,

And it's doubtful if his spirit will be 'loyal thro' it all'.

Though the bush has been romantic and it's nice to sing about,
There's a lot of patriotism that the land could do without –
Sort of british workman nonsense that shall perish in the scorn
Of the drover who is driven and the shearer who is shorn,
Of the struggling western farmers who have little time for rest,
And are ruined on selections in the sheep-infested West;
Droving songs are very pretty, but they merit little thanks
From the people of a country in possession of the Banks.

And the 'rise and fall of seasons' suits the rise and fall of rhyme,
But we know that western seasons do not run on schedule time;
For the drought will go on drying while there's anything to dry,
Then it rains until you'd fancy it would bleach the sunny sky –
Then it pelters out of reason, for the downpour day and night
Nearly sweeps the population to the Great Australian Bight.
It is up in Northern Queensland that the seasons do their best,
But it's doubtful if you ever saw a season in the West;
There are years without an autumn or a winter or a spring,
There are broiling Junes, and summers when it rains like anything.

In the bush my ears were opened to the singing of the bird,
But the 'carol of the magpie' was a thing I never heard.
Once the beggar roused my slumbers in a shanty, it is true,
But I only heard him asking, 'Who the blanky blank are you?'
And the bell-bird in the ranges – but his 'silver chime' is harsh
When it's heard beside the solo of the curlew in the marsh.

Yes, I heard the shearers singing 'William Riley', out of tune,

Saw 'em fighting round a shanty on a Sunday afternoon,

But the bushman isn't always 'trapping brumbies in the night',

Nor is he for ever riding when 'the morn is fresh and bright',

And he isn't always singing in the humpies on the run –

And the camp-fire's 'cheery blazes' are a trifle overdone;

We have grumbled with the bushmen round the fire on rainy days,

When the smoke would blind a bullock and there wasn't any blaze,

Save the blazes of our language, for we cursed the fire in turn

Till the atmosphere was heated and the wood began to burn.

Then we had to wring our blueys which were rotting in the swags,

And we saw the sugar leaking through the bottoms of the bags,

And we couldn't raise a chorus, for the toothache and the cramp,

While we spent the hours of darkness draining puddles round the camp.

Would you like to change with Clancy – go a-droving? tell us true,

For we rather think that Clancy would be glad to change with you,

And be something in the city; but 'twould give your muse a shock

To be losing time and money through the foot-rot in the flock,

And you wouldn't mind the beauties underneath the starry dome

If you had a wife and children and a lot of bills at home.

Did you ever guard the cattle when the night was inky-black,

And it rained, and icy water trickled gently down your back

Till your saddle-weary backbone fell a-aching to the roots

And you almost felt the croaking of the bull-frog in your boots –

Sit and shiver in the saddle, curse the restless stock and cough

Till a squatter's irate dummy cantered up to warn you off?

Did you fight the drought and pleuro when the 'seasons' were asleep,

Felling she-oaks all the morning for a flock of starving sheep,

Drinking mud instead of water – climbing trees and lopping boughs

For the broken-hearted bullocks and the dry and dusty cows?

Do you think the bush was better in the 'good old droving days',

When the squatter ruled supremely as the king of western ways,

When you got a slip of paper for the little you could earn,

But were forced to take provisions from the station in return –

When you couldn't keep a chicken at your humpy on the run,

For the squatter wouldn't let you – and your work was never done;

When you had to leave the missus in a lonely hut forlorn

While you 'rose up Willy Riley' – in the days ere you were born?

Ah! we read about the drovers and the shearers and the like

Till we wonder why such happy and romantic fellows strike.

Don't you fancy that the poets ought to give the bush a rest

Ere they raise a just rebellion in the over-written West?

Where the simple-minded bushman gets a meal and bed and rum

Just by riding round reporting phantom flocks that never come;

Where the scalper – never troubled by the 'war-whoop of the push' –

Has a quiet little billet – breeding rabbits in the bush;

Where the idle shanty-keeper never fails to make a draw,

And the dummy gets his tucker through provisions in the law;

Where the labour-agitator – when the shearers rise in might –

Makes his money sacrificing all his substance for The Right;

Where the squatter makes his fortune, and 'the seasons rise and fall',

And the poor and honest bushman has to suffer for it all;

Where the drovers and the shearers and the bushmen and the rest

Never reach the Eldorado of the poets of the West.

And you think the bush is purer and that life is better there,

But it doesn't seem to pay you like the 'squalid street and square'.

Pray inform us, City Bushman, where you read, in prose or verse,

Of the awful 'city urchin who would greet you with a curse'.

There are golden hearts in gutters, though their owners lack the fat,

And we'll back a teamster's offspring to outswear a city brat.

Do you think we're never jolly where the trams and buses rage?

Did you hear the gods in chorus when 'Ri-tooral' held the stage?

Did you catch a ring of sorrow in the city urchin's voice

When he yelled for Billy Elton, when he thumped the floor for Royce?

Do the bushmen, down on pleasure, miss the everlasting stars

When they drink and flirt and so on in the glow of private bars?

You've a down on 'trams and buses', or the 'roar' of 'em, you said,

And the 'filthy, dirty attic', where you never toiled for bread.

(And about that self-same attic – Lord! wherever have you been?

For the struggling needlewoman mostly keeps her attic clean.)

But you'll find it very jolly with the cuff-and-collar push,

And the city seems to suit you, while you rave about the bush.

You'll admit that Up-the Country, more especially in drought,

Isn't quite the Eldorado that the poets rave about,

Yet at times we long to gallop where the reckless bushman rides

In the wake of startled brumbies that are flying for their hides;

Long to feel the saddle tremble once again between our knees

And to hear the stockwhips rattle just like rifles in the trees!

Long to feel the bridle-leather tugging strongly in the hand

And to feel once more a little like a native of the land.

And the ring of bitter feeling in the jingling of our rhymes

Isn't suited to the country nor the spirit of the times.

Let us go together droving, and returning, if we live,

Try to understand each other while we reckon up the div.

First published in *The Bulletin*, 6 August 1892

Up THE COUNTRY

I am back from up the country – very sorry that I went,

Seeking for the Southern poets' land whereon to pitch my tent;

I have lost a lot of idols, which were broken on the track,

Burnt a lot of fancy verses, and I'm glad that I am back.

Further out may be the pleasant scenes of which our poets boast,

But I think the country's rather more inviting round the coast,

Anyway, I'll stay at present at a boarding-house in town

Drinking beer and lemon-squashes, taking baths and cooling down.

Sunny plains! Great Scot! – those burning wastes of barren soil and sand

With their everlasting fences stretching out across the land!

Desolation where the crow is! Desert where the eagle flies,

Paddocks where the luny bullock starts and stares with reddened eyes;

Where, in clouds of dust enveloped, roasted bullock-drivers creep

Slowly past the sun-dried shepherd dragged behind his crawling sheep.

Stunted 'peak' of granite gleaming, glaring like molten mass

Turned, from some infernal furnace, on a plain devoid of grass.

Miles and miles of thirsty gutters, strings of muddy waterholes

In the place of 'shining rivers' (walled by cliffs and forest boles).

Barren ridgs, gullies, ridges! where the ever madd'ning flies,

Fiercer than the plagues of Egypt, swarm about your blighted eyes!

Bush! where there is no horizon! where the buried bushman sees

Nothing. Nothing! but the maddening sameness of the stunted trees!

Lonely hut where drought's eternal, suffocating atmosphere,

Where the God forgotten hatter dreams of city-life and beer.

66

Treacherous tracks that trap the stranger, endless roads that gleam and glare,

Dark and evil-looking gullies, hiding secrets here and there!

Dull dumb flats and stony rises, where the bullocks sweat and bake,

And the sinister gohanna, and the lizard, and the snake.

Land of day and night – no morning freshness, and no afternoon,

For the great, white sun in rising brings with him the heat of noon.

Dismal country for the exile, when the shades begin to fall

From the sad, heart-breaking sunset, to the new-chum, worst of all.

Dreary land in rainy weather, with the endless clouds that drift

O'er the bushman like a blanket that the Lord will never lift –

Dismal land when it is raining – growl of floods and oh! the woosh

Of the rain and wind together on the dark bed of the bush –

Ghastly fires in lonely humpies where the granite rocks are pil'd

On the rain-swept wildernesses that are wildest of the wild.

Land where gaunt and haggard women live alone and work like men,

Till their husbands, gone a-droving, will return to them again:

Homes of men! if homes had ever such a God-forgotten place,

Where the wild selector's children fly before a stranger's face.

Home of tragedy applauded by the dingoes' dismal yell,

Heaven of the shanty-keeper – fitting fiend for such a hell –

And the wallaroos and wombats, and, of course, the curlew's call –

And the lone sundowner tramping ever onward thro' it all!

I am back from up the country, up the country where I went

Seeking for the Southern poets' land whereon to pitch my tent;

I have left a lot of broken idols out along the track,

Burnt a lot of fancy verses – and I'm glad that I am back,

I believe the Southern poet's dream will not be realised

Till the plains are irrigated and the land is humanised.

I intend to stay at present, as I said before, in town

Drinking beer and lemon-squashes, taking baths and cooling down.

First published in *The Bulletin*, 9 July 1892.

The
BUSH UNDERTAKER

'Five Bob!'

The old man shaded his eyes and peered through the dazzling glow of that broiling Christmas Day. He stood just within the door of a slab-and-bark hut situated upon the bank of a barren creek; sheep-yards lay to the right, and a low line of bare, brown ridges formed a suitable background to the scene.

'Five Bob!' shouted he again; and a dusty sheep-dog rose wearily from the shaded side of the but and looked inquiringly at his master, who pointed towards some sheep which were straggling from the flock.

'Fetch 'em back,' he said confidently.

The dog went off, and his master returned to the interior of the hut.

'We'll yard 'em early,' he said to himself; 'the super won't know. We'll yard 'em early, and have the arternoon to ourselves.'

'We'll get dinner,' he added, glancing at some pots on the fire. 'I cud do a bit of doughboy, an' that theer boggabri'll eat like tater-marrer along of the salt meat.' He moved one of the black buckets from the blaze. 'I likes to keep it jist on the sizzle,' he said in explanation to himself; 'hard bilin' makes it tough – I'll keep it jist a-simmerin'.'

Here his soliloquy was interrupted by the return of the dog.

'All right, Five Bob,' said the hatter, 'dinner'll be ready dreckly. Jist keep yer eye on the sheep till I calls yer; keep 'em well rounded up, an' we'll yard 'em afterwards and have a holiday.'

This speech was accompanied by a gesture evidently intelligible, for the dog retired as though he understood English, and the cooking proceeded.

'I'll take a pick an' shovel with me an' root up that old blackfellow,' mused the shepherd, evidently following up a recent train of thought; 'I reckon it'll do now. I'll put in the spuds.'

The last sentence referred to the cooking, the first to a blackfellow's grave about which he was curious.

'The sheep's a-campin',' said the soliloquizer, glancing through the door. 'So me an' Five Bob'll be able to get our dinner in peace. I wish I had just enough fat to make the pan siss; I'd treat myself to a leather-jacket; but it took three weeks' skimmin' to get enough for them theer doughboys.'

In due time the dinner was dished up; and the old man seated himself on a block, with the lid of a gin-case across his knees for a table. Five Bob squatted opposite with the liveliest interest and appreciation depicted on his intelligent countenance.

Dinner proceeded very quietly, except when the carver paused to ask the dog how some tasty morsel went with him, and Five Bob's tail declared that it went very well indeed.

'Here y'are, try this,' cried the old man, tossing him a large piece of doughboy. A click of Five Bob's jaws and the dough was gone.

'Clean into his liver!' said the old man with a faint smile. He washed up the tinware in the water the duff had been boiled in, and then, with the assistance of the dog, yarded the sheep.

This accomplished, he took a pick and shovel and an old sack, and started out over the ridge, followed, of course, by his four-legged mate. After tramping some three miles he reached a spur, running out from the main ridge. At the extreme end of this, under some gum-trees, was a little mound of earth, barely defined in the grass, and indented in the centre as all blackfellows' graves were.

He set to work to dig it up, and sure enough, in about half an hour he bottomed on payable dirt.

When he had raked up all the bones, he amused himself by putting them together on the grass and by speculating as to whether they had belonged to black or white, male or female. Failing, however, to arrive at any satisfactory conclusion, he dusted them with great care, put them in the bag, and started for home.

He took a short cut this time over the ridge and down a gully which was full of ring-barked trees and long white grass. He had nearly reached its mouth when a great greasy black goanna clambered up a sapling from under his feet and looked fightable.

'Dang the jumpt-up thing!' cried the old man. 'It 'gin me a start!'

At the foot of the sapling he espied an object which he at first thought was the blackened carcass of a sheep, but on closer examination discovered to be the body of a man; it lay with its forehead resting on its hands, dried to a mummy by the intense heat of the western summer.

'Me luck's in for the day and no mistake!' said the shepherd, scratching the back of his head, while he took stock of the remains. He picked up a stick and tapped the body on the shoulder; the flesh sounded like leather. He turned it over on its side; it fell flat on its back like a board, and the shrivelled eyes seemed to peer up at him from under the blackened wrists.

He stepped back involuntarily, but, recovering himself, leant on his stick and took in all the ghastly details.

There was nothing in the blackened features to tell aught of name or race, but the dress proclaimed the remains to be those of a European. The old man caught sight of a black bottle in the grass, close beside the corpse. This set him thinking. Presently he knelt down and examined the soles of the dead man's blucher boots, and then, rising with an air of conviction, exclaimed: 'Brummy! by gosh! – busted up at last!

'I tole yer so, Brummy,' he said impressively, addressing the corpse. 'I allers told yer as how it 'ud be – an' here y'are, you thundering jumpt-up cuss-o'-God fool. Yer cud earn more'n any man in the colony, but yer'd lush it all away. I allers sed as how it 'ud end, an' now yer kin see fur y'self.

'I spect yer was a-comin' t' me t' get fixt up an' set straight agin; then yer was a-goin' to swear off, same as yer 'allers did; an' here y'are, an' now I expect I'll have t' fix yer up for the last time an' make yer decent, for 'twon't do t' leave yer alyin' out here like a dead sheep.'

He picked up the corked bottle and examined it. To his great surprise it was nearly full of rum.

'Well, this gits me,' exclaimed the old man; 'me luck's in, this Christmas, an' no mistake. He must 'a' got the jams early in his spree, or he wouldn't be a-making for me with near a bottleful left. Howsomenever, here goes.'

Looking round, his eyes lit up with satisfaction as he saw some bits of bark which had been left by a party of strippers who had been getting bark there for the stations. He picked up two pieces, one about four and the other six feet long, and each about two feet wide, and brought them over to the body. He laid the longest strip by the side of the corpse, which he proceeded to lift on to it.

'Come on, Brummy,' he said, in a softer tone than usual, 'ye ain't as bad as yer might be, considerin' as it must be three good months since yer slipped yer wind. I spect it was the rum as preserved yer. It was the death of yer when yer was alive, an' now yer dead, it preserves yer like – like a mummy.'

Then he placed the other strip on top, with the hollow side downwards – thus sandwiching the defunct between the two pieces – removed the saddle-strap, which he wore for a belt, and buckled it round one end, while he tried to think of something with which to tie up the other.

'I can't take any more strips off my shirt,' he said, critically examining the skirts of the old blue overshirt he wore. 'I might get a strip or two more off, but it's short enough already. Let's see; how long have I been a-wearin' of that shirt; oh, I remember, I bought it jist two days afore Five Bob was pupped. I can't afford a new shirt jist yet; howsomenever, seein' it's Brummy, I'll jist borrow a couple more strips and sew 'em on agen when I git home.'

He up-ended Brummy, and placing his shoulder against the middle of the lower sheet of bark, lifted the corpse to a horizontal position; then, taking the bag of bones in his hand, he started for home.

'I ain't a-spendin' sech a dull Christmas arter all,' he reflected, as he plodded on; but he had not walked above a hundred yards when he saw a black goanna sidling into the grass.

'That's another of them theer dang things!' he exclaimed. 'That's two I've seed this mornin'.'

Presently he remarked: 'Yer don't smell none too sweet, Brummy. It must 'a' been jist about the middle of shearin' when yer pegged out. I wonder who got yer last cheque. Shoo! theer's another black goanner – theer must be a flock of 'em.'

He rested Brummy on the ground while he had another pull at the bottle, and, before going on, packed the bag of bones on his shoulder under the body, and he soon stopped again.

'The thunderin' jumpt-up bones is all skew-whift,' he said. "Ole on, Brummy, an' I'll fix 'em'– and he leaned the dead man against a tree while he settled the bones on his shoulder, and took another pull at the bottle.

About a mile further on he heard a rustling in the grass to the right, and, looking round, saw another goanna gliding off sideways, with its long snaky neck turned towards him.

This puzzled the shepherd considerably, the strangest part of it being that Five Bob wouldn't touch the reptile, but slunk off with his tail down when ordered to 'sick 'em.'

'Theer's sothin' comic about them theer goanners,' said the old man at last. 'I've seed swarms of grasshoppers an' big mobs of kangaroos, but dang me if ever I seed a flock of black goanners afore!'

On reaching the hut the old man dumped the corpse against the wall, wrong end up, and stood scratching his head while he endeavoured to collect his muddled thoughts; but he had not placed Brummy at the correct angle, and, consequently, that individual fell forward and struck him a violent blow on the shoulder with the iron toes of his blucher boots.

The shock sobered him. He sprang a good yard, instinctively hitching up his moleskins in preparation for flight; but a backward glance revealed to him the true cause of this supposed attack from the rear. Then he lifted the body, stood it on its feet against the chimney, and ruminated as to where he should lodge his mate for the night, not noticing that the shorter sheet of bark had slipped down on the boots and left the face exposed.

'I spect I'll have ter put yer into the chimney-trough for the night, Brummy,' said he, turning round to confront the corpse. 'Yer can't expect me to take yer into the hut, though I did it when yer was in a worse state than – Lord!'

The shepherd was not prepared for the awful scrutiny that gleamed on him from those empty sockets; his nerves received a shock, and it was some time before he recovered himself sufficiently to speak.

'Now, look a-here, Brummy,' said he, shaking his finger severely at the delinquent, 'I don't want to pick a row with yer; I'd do as much for yer an' more than any other man, an' well yer knows it; but if yer starts playin' any of yer jumpt-up pranktical jokes on me, and a-scarin' of me after a-humpin' of yer 'ome, by the 'oly frost I'll kick yer to jim-rags, so I will.'

This admonition delivered, he hoisted Brummy into the chimney-trough, and with a last glance towards the sheep-yards, he retired to his bunk to have, as he said, a snooze.

He had more than a snooze, however, for when he woke, it was dark, and the bushman's instinct told him it must be nearly nine o'clock.

He lit a slush-lamp and poured the remainder of the rum into a pannikin; but, just as he was about to lift the draught to his lips, he heard a peculiar rustling sound overhead, and put the pot down on the table with a slam that spilled some of the precious liquor.

Five Bob whimpered, and the old shepherd, though used to the weird and dismal, as one living alone in the bush must necessarily be, felt the icy breath of fear at his heart.

He reached hastily for his old shot-gun, and went out to investigate. He walked round the but several times and examined the roof on all sides, but saw nothing. Brummy appeared to be in the same position.

At last, persuading himself that the noise was caused by possums or the wind, the old man went inside, boiled his billy, and, after composing his nerves somewhat with a light supper and a meditative smoke, retired for the night. He was aroused several times before midnight by the same mysterious sound overhead, but, though he rose and examined the roof on each occasion by the light of the rising moon, he discovered nothing.

At last he determined to sit up and watch until daybreak, and for this purpose took up a position on a log a short distance from the hut, with his gun laid in readiness across his knee.

After watching for about an hour, he saw a black object coming over the ridge-pole. He grabbed his gun and fired. The thing disappeared. He ran round to the other side of the hut, and there was a great black goanna in violent convulsions on the ground.

Then the old man saw it all. 'The thunderin' jumpt-up thing has been a-havin' o' me,' he exclaimed. 'The same cuss-o'-God wretch has a-follered me 'ome, an' has been a-havin' its Christmas dinner off of Brummy, an' a-hauntin' o' me into the bargain, the jumpt-up tinker!'

As there was no one by whom he could send a message to the station, and the old man dared not leave the sheep and go himself, he determined to bury the body the next afternoon, reflecting that the authorities could disinter it for inquest if they pleased.

So he brought the sheep home early and made arrangements for the burial by measuring the outer casing of Brummy and digging a hole according to those dimensions.

'That 'minds me,' he said. 'I never rightly knowed Brummy's religion, blest if ever I did. Howsomenever, there's one thing sartin – none o' them theer pianer-fingered parsons is a-goin' ter take the trouble ter travel out inter this God-forgotten part to hold sarvice over him, seein' as how his last cheque's blued. But, as I've got the fun'ral arrangements all in me own hands, I'll do jestice to it, and see that Brummy has a good comfortable buryin'– and more's unpossible.'

'It's time yer turned in, Brum,' he said, lifting the body down.

He carried it to the grave and dropped it into one corner like a post. He arranged the bark so as to cover the face, and, by means of a piece of clothes-line, lowered the body to a horizontal position. Then he threw in an armful of gum-leaves, and then, very reluctantly, took the shovel and dropped in a few shovelfuls of earth.

'An' this is the last of Brummy,' he said, leaning on his spade and looking away over the tops of the ragged gums on the distant range.

This reflection seemed to engender a flood of memories, in which the old man became absorbed. He leaned heavily upon his spade and thought.

'Arter all,' he murmured sadly, 'arter all – it were Brummy.

'Brummy,' he said at last. 'It's all over now; nothin' matters now – nothin' didn't ever matter, nor – nor don't. You uster say as how it 'ud be all right termorrer' (pause); 'termorrer's come, Brummy – come fur you – it ain't come fur me yet, but – it's a-comin'.'

He threw in some more earth.

'Yer don't remember, Brummy, an' mebbe yer don't want to remember – I don't want to remember – but – well, but, yer see that's where yer got the pull on me.'

He shovelled in some more earth and paused again.

The dog rose, with ears erect, and looked anxiously first at his master and then into the grave.

'Theer oughter be somethin' sed,' muttered the old man; "'tain't right to put 'im under like a dog. Theer oughter be some sort o' sarmin.' He sighed heavily in the listening silence that followed this remark and proceeded with his work. He filled the grave to the brim this time, and fashioned the mound carefully with his spade. Once or twice he muttered the words, 'I am the rassaraction.' As he laid the tools quietly aside, and stood at the head of the grave, he was evidently trying to remember the something that ought to be said. He removed his hat, placed it carefully on the grass, held his hands out from his sides and a little to the front, drew a long deep breath, and said with a solemnity that greatly disturbed Five Bob: 'Hashes ter hashes, dus ter dus, Brummy – an'– an' in hopes of a great an' gerlorious rassaraction!'

He sat down on a log nearby, rested his elbows on his knees and passed his hand wearily over his forehead – but only as one who was tired and felt the heat; and presently he rose, took up the tools, and walked back to the hut.

And the sun sank again on the grand Australian bush – the nurse and tutor of eccentric minds, the home of the weird.

First published in *The Antipodean*, 1892

Saint
PETER

Now, I think there is a likeness
    'Twixt St Peter's life and mine
For he did a lot of trampin'
    Long ago in Palestine.
He was 'union' when the workers
    First began to organise,
And – I'm glad that old St Peter
    Keeps the gate of Paradise.

When the ancient agitator
   And his brothers carried swags,
I've no doubt he very often
   Tramped with empty tucker-bags;
And I'm glad he's Heaven's picket,
   For I hate explainin' things,
And he'll think a union ticket
   Just as good as Whitely King's.

He denied the Saviour's union,
   Which was weak of him, no doubt;
But perhaps his feet was blistered
   And his boots had given out.
And the bitter storm was rushin'
   On the bark and on the slabs,
And a cheerful fire was blazin',
   And the hut was full of 'scabs'.

When I reach the great head-station –
   Which is somewhere 'off the track' –
I won't want to talk with angels
   Who have never been out back ;
They might bother me with offers
   Of a banjo – meanin' well –
And a pair of wings to fly with,
   When I only want a spell.

I'll just ask for old St Peter,

    And I think, when he appears,

I will only have to tell him

    That I carried swag for years.

'I've been on the track,' I'll tell him,

    'an' I done the best I could,'

And he'll understand me better

    Than the other angels would.

He won't try to get a chorus

    Out of lungs that's worn to rags,

Or to graft the wings on shoulders

    That is stiff with humpin' swags.

But I'll rest about the station

    Where the work-bell never rings,

Till they blow the final trumpet

    And the Great Judge sees to things.

First published in 1893

Since
THEN

I met Jack Ellis in town to-day —
   Jack Ellis — my old mate, Jack —
Ten years ago, from the Castlereagh,
We carried our swags together away
   To the Never-Again, Out Back.

But times have altered since those old days,
   And the times have changed the men.
Ah, well! there's little to blame or praise —
Jack Ellis and I have tramped long ways
   On different tracks since then.

His hat was battered, his coat was green,

　The toes of his boots were through,

But the pride was his! It was I felt mean –

I wished that my collar was not so clean,

　Nor the clothes I wore so new.

He saw me first, and he knew 'twas I –

　The holiday swell he met.

Why have we no faith in each other? Ah, why? –

He made as though he would pass me by,

　For he thought that I might forget.

He ought to have known me better than that,
　　By the tracks we tramped far out –
The sweltering scrub and the blazing flat,
When the heat came down through each old felt hat
　　In the hell-born western drought.

The cheques we made and the shanty sprees,
　　The camps in the great blind scrub,
The long wet tramps when the plains were seas,
And the oracles worked in days like these
　　For rum and tobacco and grub.

Could I forget how we struck 'the same
　　Old tale' in the nearer West,
When the first great test of our friendship came –
But – well, there's little to praise or blame
　　If our mateship stood the test.

'Heads!' he laughed (but his face was stern) –
　　'Tails!' and a friendly oath;
We loved her fair, we had much to learn –
And each was stabbed to the heart in turn
　　By the girl who – loved us both.

Or the last day lost on the lignum plain,

When I staggered, half-blind, half-dead,

With a burning throat and a tortured brain;

And the tank when we came to the track again

Was seventeen miles ahead.

Then life seemed finished – then death began

As down in the dust I sank,

But he stuck to his mate as a bushman can,

Till I heard him saying, 'Bear up, old man!'

In the shade by the mulga tank.

He took my hand in a distant way

(I thought how we parted last),

And we seemed like men who have nought to say

And who meet – 'Good-day', and who part – 'Good-day',

Who never have shared the past.

I asked him in for a drink with me –

Jack Ellis – my old mate, Jack –

But his manner no longer was careless and free,

He followed, but not with the grin that he

Wore always in days Out Back.

I tried to live in the past once more –

   Or the present and past combine,

But the days between I could not ignore –

I couldn't help notice the clothes he wore,

   And he couldn't but notice mine.

He placed his glass on the polished bar,

   And he wouldn't fill up again;

For he is prouder than most men are –

Jack Ellis and I have tramped too far

   On different tracks since then.

He said that he had a mate to meet,

    And 'I'll see you again,' said he,

Then he hurried away through the crowded street

And the rattle of buses and scrape of feet

    Seemed suddenly loud to me.

And I almost wished that the time were come

    When less will be left to Fate –

When boys will start on the track from home

With equal chances, and no old chum

    Have more or less than his mate.

First published in *The Bulletin*, 23 November 1895

The MEN WE MIGHT HAVE BEEN

When God's wrath-cloud is o'er me,
   Affrighting heart and mind;
When days seem dark before me,
   And days seem black behind;
Those friends who think they know me –
   Who deem their insight keen –
They ne'er forget to show me
   The man I might have been.

He's rich and independent,
  Or rising fast to fame;
His bright star is ascendant,
  The country knows his name;
His houses and his gardens
  Are splendid to be seen;
His fault the wise world pardons –
  The man I might have been.

His fame and fortune haunt me;
  His virtues wave me back:
His name and prestige daunt me
  When I would take the track;
But you, my friend true-hearted –
  God, keep our friendship green! –
You know how I was parted
  From all I might have been.

But what avails the ache of

   Remorse or weak regret?

We'll battle for the sake of

   The men we might be yet!

We'll strive to keep in sight of

   The brave, the true and clean

And triumph yet in spite of

   The men we might have been.

First published in *The Bulletin*, 3 April 1897

The
IRON-BARK CHIP

Dave Regan and party — bush-fencers, tank-sinkers, rough carpenters, &c. — were finishing the third and last culvert of their contract on the last section of the new railway line, and had already sent in their vouchers for the completed contract, so that there might be no excuse for extra delay in connection with the cheque.

Now it had been expressly stipulated in the plans and specifications that the timber for certain beams and girders was to be iron-bark and no other, and Government inspectors were authorised to order the removal from the ground of any timber or material they might deem inferior, or not in accordance with the stipulations. The railway contractor's foreman and inspector of sub-contractors was a practical man and a bushman, but he had been a timber-getter himself; his sympathies were bushy, and he was on winking terms with Dave Regan. Besides, extended time was expiring, and the contractors were in a hurry to complete the line. But the Government inspector was a reserved man who poked round on his independent own and appeared in lonely spots at unexpected times – with apparently no definite object in life – like a grey kangaroo bothered by a new wire fence, but unsuspicious of the presence of humans. He wore a grey suit, rode, or mostly led, an ashen-grey horse; the grass was long and grey, so he was seldom spotted until he was well within the horizon and bearing leisurely down on a party of sub-contractors, leading his horse.

Now iron-bark was scarce and distant on those ridges, and another timber, similar in appearance, but much inferior in grain and 'standing' quality, was plentiful and close at hand. Dave and party were 'about full of' the job and place, and wanted to get their cheque and be gone to another 'spec' they had in view. So they came to reckon they'd get the last girder from a handy tree, and have it squared, in place, and carefully and conscientiously tarred before the inspector happened along, if he did. But they didn't. They got it squared, and ready to be lifted into its place; the kindly darkness of tar was ready to cover a fraud that took four strong men with crowbars and levers to shift; and now (such is the regular cussedness of things) as the fraudulent piece of timber lay its last hour on the ground, looking and smelling, to their guilty imaginations like anything but iron-bark, they were aware of the Government inspector drifting down upon them obliquely, with something of the atmosphere of a casual Bill or Jim who had dropped out of his easy-going track to see how they were getting on, and borrow a match. They had more than half hoped that, as he had visited them pretty frequently during the progress of the work, and knew how near it was to completion, he wouldn't bother coming any more. But it's the way with the Government. You might move heaven and earth in vain endeavour to get the 'Guvermunt' to flutter an eyelash over something of the most momentous importance to yourself and mates and the district — even to the country; but just when you are leaving authority severely alone, and have strong reasons for not wanting to worry or interrupt it, and not desiring it to worry about you, it will take a fancy into its head to come along and bother.

'It's always the way!' muttered Dave to his mates. 'I knew the beggar would turn up! . . . And the only cronk log we've had, too!' he added, in an injured tone. 'If this had 'a' been the only blessed iron-bark in the whole contract, it would have been all right. . . . Good-day, sir!' (to the inspector). 'It's hot?'

The inspector nodded. He was not of an impulsive nature. He got down from his horse and looked at the girder in an abstracted way; and presently there came into his eyes a dreamy, far-away, sad sort of expression, as if there had been a very sad and painful occurrence in his family, way back in the past, and that piece of timber in some way reminded him of it and brought the old sorrow home to him. He blinked three times, and asked, in a subdued tone:

'Is that iron-bark?'

Jack Bentley, the fluent liar of the party, caught his breath with a jerk and coughed, to cover the gasp and gain time. 'I – iron-bark? Of course it is! I thought you would know iron-bark, mister.' (Mister was silent.) 'What else d'yer think it is?'

The dreamy, abstracted expression was back. The inspector, by-the-way, didn't know much about timber, but he had a great deal of instinct, and went by it when in doubt.

'L – look here, mister!' put in Dave Regan, in a tone of innocent puzzlement and with a blank bucolic face. 'B – but don't the plans and specifications say iron-bark? Ours does, anyway. I – I'll git the papers from the tent and show yer, if yer like.'

It was not necessary. The inspector admitted the fact slowly. He stooped, and with an absent air picked up a chip. He looked at it abstractedly for a moment, blinked his threefold blink; then, seeming to recollect an appointment, he woke up suddenly and asked briskly:

'Did this chip come off that girder?'

Blank silence. The inspector blinked six times, divided in threes, rapidly, mounted his horse, said 'Day,' and rode off.

Regan and party stared at each other.

'Wha – what did he do that for?' asked Andy Page, the third in the party.

'Do what for, you fool?' enquired Dave.

'Ta – take that chip for?'

'He's taking it to the office!' snarled Jack Bentley.

'What – what for? What does he want to do that for?'

'To get it blanky well analysed! You ass! Now are yer satisfied?' And Jack sat down hard on the timber, jerked out his pipe, and said to Dave, in a sharp, toothache tone:

'Gimmiamatch!'

'We–well! what are we to do now?' enquired Andy, who was the hardest grafter, but altogether helpless, hopeless, and useless in a crisis like this.

'Grain and varnish the bloomin' culvert!' snapped Bentley.

But Dave's eyes, that had been ruefully following the inspector, suddenly dilated. The inspector had ridden a short distance along the line, dismounted, thrown the bridle over a post, laid the chip (which was too big to go in his pocket) on top of it, got through the fence, and was now walking back at an angle across the line in the direction of the fencing party, who had worked up on the other side, a little more than opposite the culvert.

Dave took in the lay of the country at a glance and thought rapidly.

'Gimme an iron-bark chip!' he said suddenly.

Bentley, who was quick-witted when the track was shown him, as is a kangaroo dog (Jack ran by sight, not scent), glanced in the line of Dave's eyes, jumped up, and got a chip about the same size as that which the inspector had taken.

Now the 'lay of the country' sloped generally to the line from both sides, and the angle between the inspector's horse, the fencing party, and the culvert was well within a clear concave space; but a couple of hundred yards back from the line and parallel to it (on the side on which Dave's party worked their timber) a fringe of scrub ran to within a few yards of a point which would be about in line with a single tree on the cleared slope, the horse, and the fencing party.

Dave took the iron-bark chip, ran along the bed of the water-course into the scrub, raced up the siding behind the bushes, got safely, though without breathing, across the exposed space, and brought the tree into line between him and the inspector, who was talking to the fencers. Then he began to work quickly down the slope towards the tree (which was a thin one), keeping it in line, his arms close to his sides, and working, as it were, down the trunk of the tree, as if the fencing party were kangaroos and Dave was trying to get a shot at them. The inspector, by-the-bye, had a habit of glancing now and then in the direction of his horse, as though under the impression that it was flighty and restless and

inclined to bolt on opportunity. It was an anxious moment for
all parties concerned – except the inspector. They didn't want
him to be perturbed. And, just as Dave reached the foot of the
tree, the inspector finished what he had to say to the fencers,
turned, and started to walk briskly back to his horse. There was
a thunderstorm coming. Now was the critical moment – there
were certain prearranged signals between Dave's party and the
fencers which might have interested the inspector, but none to
meet a case like this.

Jack Bentley gasped, and started forward with an idea of intercepting the inspector and holding him for a few minutes in bogus conversation. Inspirations come to one at a critical moment, and it flashed on Jack's mind to send Andy instead. Andy looked as innocent and guileless as he was, but was uncomfortable in the vicinity of 'funny business', and must have an honest excuse. 'Not that that mattered,' commented Jack afterwards; 'it would have taken the inspector ten minutes to get at what Andy was driving at, whatever it was.'

'Run, Andy! Tell him there's a heavy thunderstorm coming and he'd better stay in our humpy till it's over. Run! Don't stand staring like a blanky fool. He'll be gone!'

Andy started. But just then, as luck would have it, one of the fencers started after the inspector, hailing him as 'Hi, mister!' He wanted to be set right about the survey or something – or to pretend to want to be set right–from motives of policy which I haven't time to explain here.

That fencer explained afterwards to Dave's party that he 'seen what you coves was up to,' and that's why he called the inspector back. But he told them that after they had told their yarn – which was a mistake.

'Come back, Andy!' cried Jack Bentley.

Dave Regan slipped round the tree, down on his hands and knees, and made quick time through the grass which, luckily, grew pretty tall on the thirty or forty yards of slope between the tree and the horse. Close to the horse, a thought struck Dave that pulled him up, and sent a shiver along his spine and a hungry feeling under it. The horse would break away and bolt! But the case was desperate. Dave ventured an interrogatory 'Cope, cope, cope?' The horse turned its head wearily and regarded him with a mild eye, as if he'd expected him to come, and come on all fours, and wondered what had kept him so long; then he went on thinking. Dave reached the foot of the post; the horse obligingly leaning over on the other leg. Dave reared head and shoulders cautiously behind the post, like a snake; his hand went up twice, swiftly – the first time he grabbed the inspector's chip, and the second time he put the iron-bark one in its place. He drew down and back, and scuttled off for the tree like a gigantic tailless 'goanna'.

A few minutes later he walked up to the culvert from along the creek, smoking hard to settle his nerves.

The sky seemed to darken suddenly; the first great drops of the thunderstorm came pelting down. The inspector hurried to his horse, and cantered off along the line in the direction of the fettlers' camp.

He had forgotten all about the chip, and left it on top of the post! Dave Regan sat down on the beam in the rain and swore comprehensively.

First Published in *On The Track*, 1900

The
LOADED DOG

Dave Regan, Jim Bently, and Andy Page were sinking a shaft
at Stony Creek in search of a rich gold quartz reef which was
supposed to exist in the vicinity. There is always a rich reef
supposed to exist in the vicinity; the only questions are whether
it is ten feet or hundreds beneath the surface, and in which
direction. They had struck some pretty solid rock, also water
which kept them baling. They used the old-fashioned blasting-
powder and time-fuse. They'd make a sausage or cartridge of
blasting-powder in a skin of strong calico or canvas, the mouth
sewn and bound round the end of the fuse; they'd dip the
cartridge in melted tallow to make it water-tight, get the drill-
hole as dry as possible, drop in the cartridge with some dry dust,
and wad and ram with stiff clay and broken brick. Then they'd
light the fuse and get out of the hole and wait. The result was

usually an ugly pot-hole in the bottom of the shaft and half a barrow-load of broken rock.

There was plenty of fish in the creek, fresh-water bream, cod, cat-fish, and tailers. The party were fond of fish, and Andy and Dave of fishing. Andy would fish for three hours at a stretch if encouraged by a 'nibble' or a 'bite' now and then – say once in twenty minutes. The butcher was always willing to give meat in exchange for fish when they caught more than they could eat; but now it was winter, and these fish wouldn't bite. However, the creek was low, just a chain of muddy water-holes, from the hole with a few bucketfuls in it to the sizable pool with an average depth of six or seven feet, and they could get fish by baling out the smaller holes or muddying up the water in the larger ones till the fish rose to the surface. There was the cat-fish, with spikes growing out of the sides of its head, and if you got pricked you'd know it, as Dave said. Andy took off his boots, tucked up his trousers, and went into a hole one day to stir up the mud with his feet, and he knew it. Dave scooped one out with his hand and got pricked, and he knew it too; his arm swelled, and the pain throbbed up into his shoulder, and down into his stomach too, he said, like a toothache he had once, and kept him awake for two nights – only the toothache pain had a 'burred edge', Dave said.

Dave got an idea.

'Why not blow the fish up in the big water-hole with a cartridge?' he said. 'I'll try it.'

He thought the thing out and Andy Page worked it out. Andy usually put Dave's theories into practice if they were practicable, or bore the blame for the failure and the chaffing of his mates if they weren't.

He made a cartridge about three times the size of those they used in the rock. Jim Bently said it was big enough to blow the bottom out of the river. The inner skin was of stout calico; Andy stuck the end of a six-foot piece of fuse well down in the powder and bound the mouth of the bag firmly to it with whipcord. The idea was to sink the cartridge in the water with the open end of the fuse attached to a float on the surface, ready for lighting. Andy dipped the cartridge in melted bees'-wax to make it water-tight. 'We'll have to leave it some time before we light it,' said Dave, 'to give the fish time to get over their scare when we put it in, and come nosing round again; so we'll want it well water-tight.'

Round the cartridge Andy, at Dave's suggestion, bound a strip of sail canvas – that they used for making water-bags–to increase the force of the explosion, and round that he pasted layers of stiff brown paper – on the plan of the sort of fireworks we called 'gun-crackers'. He let the paper dry in the sun, then he sewed a covering of two thicknesses of canvas over it, and bound the thing from end to end with stout fishing-line. Dave's schemes were elaborate, and he often worked his inventions out to nothing. The cartridge was rigid and solid enough now – a formidable bomb; but Andy and Dave wanted to be sure. Andy sewed on another layer of canvas, dipped the cartridge in melted tallow, twisted a length of fencing-wire round it as an afterthought, dipped it in tallow again, and stood it carefully against a tent-peg, where he'd know where to find it, and wound the fuse loosely round it. Then he went to the camp-fire to try some potatoes which were boiling in their jackets in a billy, and to see about frying some chops for dinner. Dave and Jim were at work in the claim that morning.

They had a big black young retriever dog – or rather an overgrown pup, a big, foolish, four-footed mate, who was always slobbering round them and lashing their legs with his heavy tail that swung round like a stock-whip. Most of his head was usually a red, idiotic, slobbering grin of appreciation of his own silliness. He seemed to take life, the world, his two-legged mates, and his own instinct as a huge joke. He'd retrieve anything: he carted back most of the camp rubbish that Andy threw away. They had a cat that died in hot weather, and Andy threw it a good distance away in the scrub; and early one morning the dog found the cat, after it had been dead a week or so, and carried it back to camp, and laid it just inside the tent-flaps, where it could best make its presence known when the mates should rise and begin to sniff suspiciously in the sickly smothering atmosphere of the summer sunrise. He used to retrieve them when they went in swimming; he'd jump in after them, and take their hands in his mouth, and try to swim out with them, and scratch their naked bodies with his paws. They loved him for his good-heartedness and his foolishness, but when they wished to enjoy a swim they had to tie him up in camp.

He watched Andy with great interest all the morning making the cartridge, and hindered him considerably, trying to help; but about noon he went off to the claim to see how Dave and Jim were getting on, and to come home to dinner with them. Andy saw them coming, and put a panful of mutton-chops on the fire. Andy was cook to-day; Dave and Jim stood with their backs to the fire, as Bushmen do in all weathers, waiting till dinner should be ready. The retriever went nosing round after something he seemed to have missed.

Andy's brain still worked on the cartridge; his eye was caught by the glare of an empty kerosene-tin lying in the bushes, and it struck him that it wouldn't be a bad idea to sink the cartridge packed with clay, sand, or stones in the tin, to increase the force of the explosion. He may have been all out, from a scientific point of view, but the notion looked all right to him. Jim Bently, by the way, wasn't interested in their 'damned silliness'. Andy noticed an empty treacle-tin – the sort with the little tin neck or spout soldered on to the top for the convenience of pouring out the treacle – and it struck him that this would have made the best kind of cartridge-case: he would only have had to pour in the powder, stick the fuse in through the neck, and cork and seal it with bees'-wax. He was turning to suggest this to Dave, when Dave glanced over his shoulder to see how the chops were doing – and bolted. He explained afterwards that he thought he heard the pan spluttering extra, and looked to see if the chops were burning. Jim Bently looked behind and bolted after Dave. Andy stood stock-still, staring after them.

'Run, Andy! run!' they shouted back at him. 'Run!!! Look behind you, you fool!' Andy turned slowly and looked, and there, close behind him, was the retriever with the cartridge in his mouth– wedged into his broadest and silliest grin. And that wasn't all. The dog had come round the fire to Andy, and the loose end of

the fuse had trailed and waggled over the burning sticks into the blaze; Andy had slit and nicked the firing end of the fuse well, and now it was hissing and spitting properly.

Andy's legs started with a jolt; his legs started before his brain did, and he made after Dave and Jim. And the dog followed Andy.

Dave and Jim were good runners – Jim the best – for a short distance; Andy was slow and heavy, but he had the strength and the wind and could last. The dog leapt and capered round him, delighted as a dog could be to find his mates, as he thought, on for a frolic. Dave and Jim kept shouting back, 'Don't foller us! don't foller us, you coloured fool!' but Andy kept on, no matter how they dodged. They could never explain, any more than the dog, why they followed each other, but so they ran, Dave keeping in Jim's track in all its turnings, Andy after Dave, and the dog circling round Andy – the live fuse swishing in all directions and hissing and spluttering and stinking. Jim yelling to Dave not to follow him, Dave shouting to Andy to go in another direction – to 'spread out', and Andy roaring at the dog to go home. Then Andy's brain began to work, stimulated by the crisis: he tried to get a running kick at the dog, but the dog dodged; he snatched up sticks and stones and threw them at the dog and ran on again. The retriever saw that he'd made a mistake about

Andy, and left him and bounded after Dave. Dave, who had the presence of mind to think that the fuse's time wasn't up yet, made a dive and a grab for the dog, caught him by the tail, and as he swung round snatched the cartridge out of his mouth and flung it as far as he could: the dog immediately bounded after it and retrieved it. Dave roared and cursed at the dog, who seeing that Dave was offended, left him and went after Jim, who was well ahead. Jim swung to a sapling and went up it like a native bear; it was a young sapling, and Jim couldn't safely get more than ten or twelve feet from the ground. The dog laid the cartridge, as carefully as if it was a kitten, at the foot of the sapling, and capered and leaped and whooped joyously round under Jim. The big pup reckoned that this was part of the lark – he was all right now – it was Jim who was out for a spree. The fuse sounded as if it were going a mile a minute. Jim tried to climb higher and the sapling bent and cracked. Jim fell on his feet and ran. The dog swooped on the cartridge and followed. It all took but a very few moments. Jim ran to a digger's hole, about ten feet deep, and dropped down into it – landing on soft mud – and was safe. The dog grinned sardonically down on him, over the edge, for a moment, as if he thought it would be a good lark to drop the cartridge down on Jim.

'Go away, Tommy,' said Jim feebly, 'go away.'

The dog bounded off after Dave, who was the only one in sight now; Andy had dropped behind a log, where he lay flat on his face, having suddenly remembered a picture of the Russo-Turkish war with a circle of Turks lying flat on their faces (as if they were ashamed) round a newly-arrived shell.

There was a small hotel or shanty on the creek, on the main road, not far from the claim. Dave was desperate, the time flew much faster in his stimulated imagination than it did in reality, so he made for the shanty. There were several casual Bushmen on the verandah and in the bar; Dave rushed into the bar, banging the door to behind him. 'My dog!' he gasped, in reply to the astonished stare of the publican, 'the blanky retriever – he's got a live cartridge in his mouth – '

The retriever, finding the front door shut against him, had bounded round and in by the back way, and now stood smiling in the doorway leading from the passage, the cartridge still in his mouth and the fuse spluttering. They burst out of that bar. Tommy bounded first after one and then after another, for, being a young dog, he tried to make friends with everybody.

The Bushmen ran round corners, and some shut themselves in the stable. There was a new weather-board and corrugated-iron kitchen and wash-house on piles in the back-yard, with some women washing clothes inside. Dave and the publican bundled in there and shut the door — the publican cursing Dave and calling him a crimson fool, in hurried tones, and wanting to know what the hell he came here for.

The retriever went in under the kitchen, amongst the piles, but, luckily for those inside, there was a vicious yellow mongrel cattle-dog sulking and nursing his nastiness under there — a sneaking, fighting, thieving canine, whom neighbours had tried for years to shoot or poison. Tommy saw his danger — he'd had experience from this dog — and started out and across the yard, still sticking to the cartridge. Half-way across the yard the yellow dog caught him and nipped him. Tommy dropped the cartridge, gave one terrified yell, and took to the Bush. The yellow dog followed him to the fence and then ran back to see what he had dropped.

Nearly a dozen other dogs came from round all the corners and under the buildings — spidery, thievish, cold-blooded kangaroo-dogs, mongrel sheep-and cattle-dogs, vicious black and yellow dogs—that slip after you in the dark, nip your heels, and vanish without explaining — and yapping, yelping small fry. They kept at a respectable distance round the nasty yellow dog, for it was dangerous to go near him when he thought he had found

something which might be good for a dog to eat. He sniffed at the cartridge twice, and was just taking a third cautious sniff when –

It was very good blasting powder – a new brand that Dave had recently got up from Sydney; and the cartridge had been excellently well made. Andy was very patient and painstaking in all he did, and nearly as handy as the average sailor with needles, twine, canvas, and rope.

Bushmen say that that kitchen jumped off its piles and on again. When the smoke and dust cleared away, the remains of the nasty yellow dog were lying against the paling fence of the yard looking

as if he had been kicked into a fire by a horse and afterwards
rolled in the dust under a barrow, and finally thrown against the
fence from a distance. Several saddle-horses, which had been
'hanging-up' round the verandah, were galloping wildly down the
road in clouds of dust, with broken bridle-reins flying; and from a
circle round the outskirts, from every point of the compass in the
scrub, came the yelping of dogs. Two of them went home, to the

place where they were born, thirty miles away, and reached it the same night and stayed there; it was not till towards evening that the rest came back cautiously to make inquiries. One was trying to walk on two legs, and most of 'em looked more or less singed; and a little, singed, stumpy-tailed dog, who had been in the habit of hopping the back half of him along on one leg, had reason to be glad that he'd saved up the other leg all those years, for he needed it now. There was one old one-eyed cattle-dog round that shanty for years afterwards, who couldn't stand the smell of a gun being cleaned. He it was who had taken an interest, only second to that of the yellow dog, in the cartridge. Bushmen said that it was amusing to slip up on his blind side and stick a dirty ramrod under his nose: he wouldn't wait to bring his solitary eye to bear – he'd take to the Bush and stay out all night.

For half an hour or so after the explosion there were several Bushmen round behind the stable who crouched, doubled up, against the wall, or rolled gently on the dust, trying to laugh without shrieking. There were two white women in hysterics at the house, and a half-caste rushing aimlessly round with a dipper of cold water. The publican was holding his wife tight and begging her between her squawks, to 'hold up for my sake, Mary, or I'll lam the life out of ye.'

Dave decided to apologise later on, 'when things had settled a bit,' and went back to camp. And the dog that had done it all, 'Tommy', the great, idiotic mongrel retriever, came slobbering round Dave and lashing his legs with his tail, and trotted home after him, smiling his broadest, longest, and reddest smile of amiability, and apparently satisfied for one afternoon with the fun he'd had.

Andy chained the dog up securely, and cooked some more chops, while Dave went to help Jim out of the hole.

And most of this is why, for years afterwards, lanky, easy-going Bushmen, riding lazily past Dave's camp, would cry, in a lazy drawl and with just a hint of the nasal twang–

''El-lo, Da-a-ve! How's the fishin' getting on, Da-a-ve?'

First published in *Joe Wilson and His Mates*, 1901

A Child
IN THE DARK,
AND A FOREIGN FATHER

NEW Year's Eve! A hot night in midsummer in the drought. It
was so dark – with a smothering darkness – that even the low
loom of the scrub-covered ridges, close at hand across the creek,
was not to be seen. The sky was not clouded for rain, but with
drought haze and the smoke of distant bush fires.

Down the hard road to the crossing at Pipeclay Creek sounded the footsteps of a man. Not the crunching steps of an English labourer, clod-hopping contentedly home; these sounded more like the footsteps of one pacing steadily to and fro, and thinking steadily and hopelessly – sorting out the past. Only the steps went on. A glimmer of white moleskin trousers and a suggestion of light-coloured tweed jacket, now and again, as if in the glimmer of a faint ghost light in the darkness.

The road ran along by the foot of a line of low ridges, or spurs, and, as he passed the gullies or gaps, he felt a breath of hotter air, like blasts from a furnace in the suffocating atmosphere. He followed a two-railed fence for a short distance, and turned in at a white batten gate. It seemed lighter now. There was a house, or, rather, a hut suggested, with whitewashed slab walls and a bark roof. He walked quietly round to the door of a detached kitchen, opened it softly, went in and struck a match. A candle stood, stuck in a blot of its own grease, on one end of the dresser. He lit the candle and looked round.

The walls of the kitchen were of split slabs, the roof box-bark, the floor clay, and there was a large clay-lined fireplace, the sides a dirty brown, and the back black. It had evidently never been whitewashed. There was a bed of about a week's ashes, and above it, suspended by a blackened hook and chain from a grimy cross-bar, hung a black bucket full of warm water. The man got a fork, explored the bucket, and found what he expected – a piece of raw corned-beef in water, which had gone off the boil before the meat had been heated through.

The kitchen was furnished with a pine table, a well-made flour bin, and a neat safe and side-board, or dresser evidently – the work of a carpenter. The top of the safe was dirty – covered with crumbs and grease and tea stains. On one corner lay a school exercise book, with a stone ink-bottle and a pen beside it. The book was open at a page written in the form of verse, in a woman's hand, and headed –

'Misunderstood.'

He took the edges of the book between his fingers and thumbs, and made to tear it, but, the cover being tough, and resisting the first savage tug, he altered his mind, and put the book down.

Then he turned to the table. There was a jumble of dirty crockery on one end, and on the other, set on a sheet of stained newspaper, the remains of a meal – a junk of badly-hacked bread, a basin of dripping (with the fat over the edges), and a tin of treacle. The treacle had run down the sides of the tin on to the paper. Knives, heavy with treacle, lay glued to the paper. There was a dish with some water, a rag, and a cup or two in it – evidently an attempt to wash-up.

The man took up a cup and pressed it hard between his palms, until it broke. Then he felt relieved. He gathered the fragments in one hand, took the candle, and stumbled out to where there was a dust-heap. Kicking a hole in the ashes, he dropped in the bits of broken crockery, and covered them. Then his anger blazed again. He walked quickly to the back door of the house, thrust the door open, and flung in, but a child's voice said from the dark –

'Is that you, father? Don't tread on me, father.'

The room was nearly as bare as the kitchen. There was a table, covered with cheap American oilcloth, and, on the other side, a sofa on which a straw mattress, a cloudy blanket, and a pillow without a slip had been thrown in a heap. On the floor, between the sofa and the table, lay a boy child almost on a similar mattress, with a cover of coarse sacking, and a bundle of dirty clothes for a pillow. A pale, thin-faced, dark-eyed boy.

'What are you doing here, sonny?' asked the father.

'Mother's bad again with her head. She says to tell you to come in quiet, and sleep on the sofa tonight. I started to wash up and clean up the kitchen, father, but I got sick.'

'Why, what is the matter with you, sonny?' His voice quickened, and he held the candle down to the child's face.

'Oh, nothing much, father. I felt sick, but I feel better now.'

'What have you been eating?'

'Nothing that I know of; I think it was the hot weather, father.'

The father spread the mattress, blew out the candle, and lay down in his clothes. After a while the boy began to toss restlessly.

'Oh, it's too hot, father,' he said. 'I'm smothering.'

The father got up, lit the candle, took a corner of the newspaper-covered 'scrim' lining that screened the cracks of the slab wall, and tore it away; then he propped open the door with a chair.

'Oh, that's better already, father,' said the boy.

The hut was three rooms long and one deep, with a veranda in front and a skillion, harness and tool room, about half the length, behind. The father opened the door of the next room softly, and propped that open, too. There was another boy on the sofa, younger than the first, but healthy and sturdy-looking. He had nothing on him but a very dirty shirt, a patchwork quilt was slipping from under him, and most of it was on the floor; the boy and the pillow were nearly off, too.

The father fixed him as comfortably as possible, and put some chairs by the sofa to keep him from rolling off. He noticed that somebody had started to scrub this room, and left it. He listened at the door of the third room for a few moments to the breathing within; then he opened it and gently walked in. There was an old-fashioned four-poster cedar bedstead, a chest of drawers, and a baby's cradle made out of a gin-case. The woman was fast asleep. She was a big, strong, and healthy-looking woman, with dark hair and strong, square features. There was a plate, a knife and fork, and egg-shells, and a cup and saucer on the top of the chest of drawers; also two candles, one stuck in a mustard tin, and one in a pickle bottle, and a copy of *Ardath*.

He stepped out into the skillion, and lifted some harness on to its pegs from chaff-bags in the corner. Coming in again, he nearly stumbled over a bucket half-full of dirty water on the floor, with a scrubbing brush, some wet rags, and half a bar of yellow soap beside it. He put these things in the bucket, and carried it out. As he passed through the first room the sick boy said –

'I couldn't lift the saddle of the harness on to the peg, father. I had to leave the scrubbing to make some tea and cook some eggs for mother, and put baby to bed, and then I felt too bad to go on with the scrubbing – and I forgot about the bucket.'

'Did the baby have any tea, sonny?'

'Yes. I made her bread and milk, and she ate a big plateful. The calves are in the pen alright, and I fixed the gate. And I brought a load of wood this morning, father, before mother took bad.'

'You should not have done that. I told you not to. I could have done that on Sunday. Now, are you sure you didn't lift a log into the cart that was too heavy for you?'

'Quite sure, father. Oh, I'm plenty strong enough to put a load of wood on the cart.'

The father lay on his back on the sofa, with his hands behind his head, for a few minutes.

'Aren't you tired, father?' asked the boy.

'No, sonny, not very tired; you must try and go to sleep now,' and he reached across the table for the candle, and blew it out.

Presently the baby cried, and in a moment the mother's voice was heard.

'Nils! Nils! Are you there, Nils?'

'Yes, Emma.'

'Then for God's sake come and take this child away before she drives me mad! My head's splitting.'

The father went in to the child and presently returned for a cup of water.

'She only wanted a drink,' the boy heard him say to the mother.

'Well, didn't I tell you she wanted a drink? I've been calling for the last half-hour, with that child screaming, and not a soul to come near me, and me lying here helpless all day, and not a wink of sleep for two nights.'

'But, Emma, you were asleep when I came in.'

'How can you tell such infernal lies? I − . To think I'm chained to a man who can't say a word of truth! God help me! To have to lie night after night in the same bed with a liar!'

The child in the first room lay quaking with terror, dreading one of those cruel and shameful scenes which had made a hell of his childhood.

'Hush, Emma!' the man kept saying. 'Do be reasonable. Think of the children. They'll hear us.'

'I don't care if they do. They'll know soon enough, God knows! I wish I was under the turf!'

'Emma, do be reasonable.'

'Reasonable! I –'

The child was crying again. The father came back to the first room, got something from his coat pocket, and took it in.

'Nils, are you quite mad, or do you want to drive me mad? Don't give the child that rattle! You must be either mad or a brute, and my nerves in this state. Haven't you got the slightest consideration for – '

'It's not a rattle, Emma; it's a doll.'

'There you go again! Flinging your money away on rubbish that'll be on the dust-heap tomorrow, and your poor wife slaving her finger-nails off for you in this wretched hole, and not a decent rag to her back. Me, your clever wife that ought to be – . Light those candles and bring me a wet towel for my head. I must read now, and try and compose my nerves, if I can.'

When the father returned to the first room, the boy was sitting up in bed, looking deathly white.

'Why, what's the matter, sonny?' said the father, bending over him, and putting a hand to his back.

'Nothing, father. I'll be all right directly. Don't you worry, father.'

'Where do you feel bad, sonny?'

'In my head and stomach, father; but I'll be all right d'rectly. I've often been that way.'

In a minute or two he was worse.

'For God's sake, Nils, take that boy into the kitchen, or somewhere,' cried the woman, 'or I'll go mad. It's enough to kill a horse. Do you want to drive me into a lunatic asylum?'

'Do you feel better now, sonny?' asked the father.

'Yes, ever so much better, father,' said the boy, white and weak. 'I'll be all right in a minute, father.'

'You had best sleep on the sofa tonight, sonny. It's cooler there.'

'No, father, I'd rather stay here; it's much cooler now.'

The father fixed the bed as comfortably as he could, and, despite the boy's protest, put his own pillow under his head. Then he made a fire in the kitchen, and hung the kettle and a big billy of water over it. He was haunted by recollections of convulsions amongst the children while they were teething. He took off his boots, and was about to lie down again when the mother called –

'Nils, Nils, have you made a fire?'

'Yes, Emma.'

'Then for God's sake make me a cup of tea. I must have it after all this.'

He hurried up the kettle – she calling every few minutes to know if 'that kettle was boiling yet.' He took her a cup of tea, and then a second. She said the tea was slush, and as sweet as syrup, and called for more, and hot water.

'How do you feel now, sonny?' he asked as he lay down on the
sofa once more.

'Much better, father. You can put out the light now if you like.'

The father blew out the candle, and settled back again, still
dressed, save for his coat, and presently the small, weak hand
sought the hard, strong, horny, knotted one; and so they lay, as was
customary with them. After a while the father leaned over a little
and whispered –

'Asleep, sonny?'

'No, father.'

'Feel bad again?'

'No, father.'

Pause.

'What are you thinking about, sonny?'

'Nothing, father.'

'But what is it? What are you worrying about? Tell me.'

'Nothing, father, only – it'll be a good while yet before I grow up to be a man, won't it, father?'

The father lay silent and troubled for a few moments.

'Why do you ask me that question to-night, sonny? I thought you'd done with all that. You were always asking me that question when you were a child. You're getting too old for those foolish fancies now. Why have you always had such a horror of growing up to be a man?'

'I don't know, father. I always had funny thoughts—you know, father. I used to think that I'd been a child once before, and grew up to be a man, and grew old and died.'

'You're not well tonight, sonny – that's what's the matter. You're queer, sonny; it's a touch of sun – that's all. Now, try to go to sleep. You'll grow up to be a man, in spite of laying awake worrying about it. If you do, you'll be a man all the sooner.'

Suddenly the mother called out –

'Can't you be quiet? What do you mean by talking at this hour of the night? Am I never to get another wink of sleep? Shut those doors, Nils, for God's sake, if you don't want to drive me mad —and make that boy hold his tongue!'

The father closed the doors.

'Better try to go to sleep now, sonny,' he whispered, as he lay down again.

The father waited for some time, then, moving very softly, he lit the candle at the kitchen fire, put it where it shouldn't light the boy's face, and watched him. And the child knew he was watching him, and pretended to sleep, and, so pretending, he slept. And the old year died as many old years had died.

The father was up about four o'clock – he worked at his trade in a farming town about five miles away, and was struggling to make a farm and a home between jobs. He cooked bacon for breakfast, washed up the dishes and tidied the kitchen, gave the boys some bread and bacon fat, of which they were very fond, and told the eldest to take a cup of tea and some bread and milk to his mother and the baby when they woke.

The boy milked the three cows, set the milk, and heard his mother calling –

'Nils! Nils!'

'Yes, mother.'

'Why didn't you answer me when I called you? I've been calling here for the last three hours. Is your father gone out?'

'Yes, mother.'

'Thank God! It's a relief to be rid of his everlasting growling. Bring me a cup of tea and the *Australian Journal*, and take this child out and dress her; she should have been up hours ago.'

And so the New Year began.

First published in *The Bulletin*, 13 December 1902

The
HEART OF AUSTRALIA

When the wars of the world seemed ended, and silent the distant drum,

Ten years ago in Australia, I wrote of a war to come:

And I pictured Australians fighting as their fathers fought of old

For the old things, pride or country, for God or the Devil or gold.

And they lounged on the rim of Australia in the peace that had come to last,

And they laughed at my 'cavalry charges' for such things belonged to the past;

Then our wise men smiled with indulgence – ere the swift years proved me right

Saying: 'What shall Australia fight for? And whom shall Australia fight?'

I wrote of the unlocked rivers in the days when my heart was full,

And I pleaded for irrigation where they sacrifice all for wool.

I pictured Australia fighting when the coast had been lost and won –

With arsenals west of the mountains and every spur its gun.

And what shall Australia fight for? The reason may yet be found,

When strange shells scatter the wickets and burst on the football ground.

And 'Who shall invade Australia?' let the wisdom of ages say

'The friend of a further future – or the ally of yesterday!'

Aye! What must Australia fight for? In the strife that never shall cease,

She must fight for her work unfinished: she must fight for her life and peace,

For the sins of the older nations. She must fight for her own reward.

She has taken the sword in her blindness and shall live or die by the sword.

But the statesman, the churchman, the scholar still peer through their glasses dim

And they see no cloud on the future as they roost on Australia's rim:

Where the farmer works with the lumpers and the drover drives a dray,

And the shearer on Garden Island is shifting a hill to-day.

Had we used the wealth we have squandered and the land that we kept from the plough,

A prosperous Federal City would be over the mountains now,

With farms that sweep to horizons and gardens where plains lay bare,

And the bulk of the population and the Heart of Australia there.

Had we used the time we have wasted and the gold we have thrown away,

The pick of the world's mechanics would be over the range to-day –

In the Valley of Coal and Iron where the breeze from the bush comes down,

And where thousands of makers of all things should be happy in Factory Town.

They droned on the rim of Australia, the wise men who never could learn;

Our substance we sent to the nations, and their shoddy we bought in return.

In the end, shall our soldiers fight naked, no help for them under the sun –

And never a cartridge to stick in the breech of a Brummagem gun?

With the Wars of the World coming near us the wise men are waking to-day.

Hurry out ammunition from England! Mount guns on the cliffs while you may!

And God pardon our sins as a people if Invasion's unmerciful hand

Should strike at the heart of Australia drought-cramped on the verge of the land.

First published in 1904

The LAST REVIEW

Turn the light down, nurse, and leave me, while I hold my last review,

For the Bush is slipping from me, and the town is going too:

Draw the blinds, the streets are lighted, and I hear the tramp of feet–

And I'm weary, very weary, of the Faces in the Street.

In the dens of Grind and Heartbreak, in the streets of Never-Rest,

I have lost the scent and colour and the music of the West:

And I would recall old faces with the memories they bring –

Where are Bill and Jim and Mary and the songs They used to Sing?

They are coming! They are coming! they are passing through the room

With the smell of gum leaves burning, and the scent of Wattle bloom!

And behind them in the timber, after dust and heat and toil,

Others sit beside the camp fire yarning while the billies boil.

In the gap above the ridges, there's a flash and there's a glow;

Swiftly down the scrub-clad siding come the Lights of Cobb and Co.:

Red face from the box-seat beaming – Oh, how plain those faces come!

From his 'Golden-Hole' 'tis Peter M'Intosh who's going home.

Dusty patch in desolation, bare slab walls and earthen floor,

And a blinding drought is blazing from horizons unto door;

Milkless tea and ration sugar, damper junk, and pumpkin mash –

And a Day on Our Selection passes by me in a flash.

Rush of big wild-eyed store bullocks while the sheep crawl hopelessly –

And the loaded wool teams rolling, lurching on like ships at sea:

With his whip across his shoulder (and the wind just now abeam),

There goes Jimmy Nowlett, ploughing through the dust beside his team!

Sunrise on the diggings! (Oh! what Life and hearts and hopes are here)

From a hundred pointing forges comes a 'tinkle-tinkle' clear –

Strings of drays with wash to puddle, clack of countless windlass boles,

Here and there the red flag flying, flying over golden holes.

Picturesque, unreal, romantic, chivalrous, and brave and free;

Clean in living, true in mateship – reckless generosity.

Mates are buried here as comrades who on fields of battle fall; –

And – the dreams, the aching, hoping lover hearts beneath it all;

Rough-built theatres and stages where the world's best actors trod –
Singers bringing reckless rovers nearer boyhood, home and God;
Paid in laughter, tears and nuggets in the play that fortune plays –
'Tis the palmy days of Gulgong – Gulgong in the Roaring Days.

Pass the same old scenes before me, and again my heart can ache:
There the Drover's Wife sits watching (not as Eve did) for a snake.
And I see the drear deserted goldfields when the night is late,
And the stony face of Mason watching by his Father's Mate.

And I see my Haggard Women plainly as they were in life,
'Tis the form of Mrs. Spicer and her friend, Joe Wilson's Wife,
Sitting hand in hand 'Past Carin',' not a sigh and not a frown,
Staring steadily before her, and the tears just trickle down.

It was No Place for a Woman – where the women worked like men –
From the Bush and Jones' Alley come their haunting forms again.
And let this thing be remembered when I've answered to the roll,
That I pitied haggard women – wrote for them with all my soul.

Narrow bedroom in the City in the hard days that are dead,
An alarm clock on the table, and a pale boy on the bed:
'Arvie Aspinall's Alarm Clock' with its harsh and startling call,
Never more shall break his slumbers – *I* was Arvie Aspinall.

Maoriland and Steelman, cynic, spieler, stiff-lipped, battler-through
Kept a wife and child in comfort, but of course they never knew –
Thought he was an honest bagman. Well, old man, you needn't hug –
Sentimental; you of all men! – Steelman, Oh! I *was* a mug!

Ghostly lines of scrub at daybreak – dusty daybreak in the drought
And a lonely swagman tramping on the track to Further Out:
Like a shade the form of Mitchell, nose-bag full and bluey up
And between the swag and shoulders lolls his foolish cattle-pup.

Kindly cynic, sad comedian! Mitchell! when you've left the rack,
And have shed your load of sorrow as we slipped our swags out-back,
We shall have a yarn together in the land of Rest Awhile –
And across his ragged shoulder Mitchell smiles his quiet smile.

Shearing sheds and tracks and shanties – girls that wait at homestead gates –
Camps and stern-eyed Union leaders, and Joe Wilson and his Mates
True and straight, and to my fancy, each one as he passes through
Deftly down upon the table slips a dusty 'note' or two.

So at last the end has found me – (end of all the human push)

And again in silence round me come my Children of the Bush!

Listen, who are young, and let them – if I, in late and bitter days,

Wrote some reckless lines – forget them – there is little there to praise.

I was human, very human, and if in the days misspent

I have injured man or woman, it was done without intent.

If at times I blundered blindly – bitter heart and aching brow –

If I wrote a line unkindly – I am sorry for it now.

Days in London lke a nightmare – dreams of foreign lands and sea –

And Australia is the only land that seemeth real to me.

Tell the bushmen to Australia and each other to be true –

'Tell the boys to stick together!' – I have held my Last Review.

First published in The Bulletin, 29 September 1904

The
LOVABLE CHARACTERS

I long for the streets but the Lord knoweth best,

    For there I am never a saint;

There are lovable characters out in the West,

    with humour heroic and quaint;

And, be it Up Country, or be it Out Back,

    When I shall have gone to my Home,

I trust to be buried 'twixt River and Track

    Where my lovable characters roam.

There are lovable characters drag through the scrub,

Where the Optimist ever prevails;
There are lovable characters hang round the pub,
  There are lovable jokers at sales
Where the auctioneer's one of the lovable wags
  (Maybe from his 'order' estranged),
And the beer is on tap, and the pigs in the bags
  Of the purchasing cockies are changed.

There are lovable characters out in the West,
  Of fifty hot summers, or more,
Who could not be proved, when it came to the test,
  Too old to be sent to the war;
They were all forty-five and were orphans, they said,
  With no one to keep them, or keep;
And mostly in France, with the world's bravest dead,
  Those lovable characters sleep.

I long for the streets but the Lord knoweth best,
  For there I am never a saint;
There are lovable characters out in the West,
  with humour heroic and quaint;
And, be it Up Country, or be it Out Back,
  When I shall have gone to my Home,
I trust to be buried 'twixt River and Track
  Where my lovable characters roam.

First published in *The Bulletin*, 8 February 1917

Index of First Lines